Lost Restaurants

OF

PHILADELPHIA

Lost Restaurants

OF

PHILADELPHIA

Amy Strauss

AMERICAN PALATE

Published by American Palate
A Division of The History Press
Charleston, SC
www.historypress.com

First published 2022

Manufactured in the United States

ISBN 9781467141758

Library of Congress Control Number: 2022935421

*For my husband, Mat, and brothers, Joel and James,
for their endless support and encouragement.*

Contents

PART V. THE ORIGINALS

PART VI. MEMORABLE RESTAURATEURS WHO SET A NEW CULINARY PACE

PART VII. UNFORGETTABLE COMFORT FOOD CLASSICS

PART VIII. SOUTH PHILLY ITALIAN KINGPINS

PART IX. ICONIC STEAKHOUSE CHARM

CONTENTS

Acknowledgements

I t brings me joy to be able to share the stories of my neighbors from years past. Food has always been an integral part of Philadelphia's DNA, and I am humbled to be given the platform of sharing these blasts from the past through Arcadia Publishing and the impressive History Press team. Complete and utter appreciation be given to my editor, Banks Smither, for this opportunity and his patience as I completed this book, as well as my production editor, Abigail Fleming, for her fabulous collaboration and keen eye to detail through the editing process. Thank you to my family, my husband and my friends, who were so encouraging to me as I worked through this writing project—I would not have been able to do what I do without your support.

I would like to also thank every restaurateur, chef and ambitious city dweller who took a chance on themselves and the City of Brotherly Love and opened up a business of their own to delight our taste buds and senses. Sincere gratitude be especially given to the city's army of talented food writers and critics, who through the years put their palates to the test to share their robust, diverse opinions of our ever-evolving food scene and the chefs who were on the frontline. Their experiences and stories are the foundation of this book, and I hope I did your words justice as I stitched them into the retellings of these iconic, defining restaurants of Philadelphia.

While the pages ahead were scribed prior to our dear city facing COVID-19, I recognize that the worldwide pandemic was incredibly taxing on the state of the restaurant industry. For those who adapted and fought hard to maintain their businesses, as well as those who painfully closed their doors, I celebrate you. Your restaurants hold fond memories for many of us of a simpler time that once was, which we will never take for granted again.

Introduction

Long before Philadelphia's food scene was splashed on covers of *Bon Appétit* magazine and regional chefs and restaurants garnered accolades like "America's best restaurant," there were the culinary pioneers that set the City of Brotherly Love's restaurant industry ablaze. In a plentiful landscape of cheesesteaks, soft pretzels and hoagies, there were chefs and restaurateurs who took risks and challenged expectations to put forth unforgettable meals—some of which were executed with cutting-edge techniques—that were well before their time.

From Frenchman Georges Perrier, who brought the city the opulent Le Bec-Fin, to Steven Poses, who changed the culinary game with the Frog, which captivated palates with the infusion of international flavors. Let us not forget the ultimate seafood institute, Old Original Bookbinder's, which held the title of the world's largest lobster tank and prepared impeccable Oysters Rockefeller, and the nation's very first Automat, the vending machine–controlled Horn & Hardart's, which drove home the finest example of consistency through near-perfect comfort food classics.

In 1976, the *Philadelphia Inquirer* published a piece suggesting that folks as far as the West Coast and as near as New York and Connecticut would travel to Philadelphia because its restaurants were their "favorite in the whole world." This gave first proof that Philadelphia was rising in its culinary reputation.

"I used to hear people say, 'I dine in New York and eat in Philadelphia,'" wrote the former *Inquirer* food critic Elaine Tait, who started her Philly critic career telling people where *not* to eat in the city. "It was only in 1979 that the whole country had begun to become aware of what we were calling our 'restaurant renaissance.' What had started with a few storefronts, some hanging plants and the courage to mix cuisines has grown into dozens of restaurants offering everything from the subtlety of haute cuisine to the directness of soul food."

And Philadelphia continues to come a long way, especially shedding the legendary epitaph W.C. Fields proposed for himself that read: "On the whole, I'd rather be in Philadelphia." There were—and are—a lot of jokes about this city. For a while you couldn't get a drink on Sunday, or a "decent" meal any day. But jokes die hard. And Philadelphia continues to earn its pedigree with a vengeance.

"Eating [in Philadelphia] is like a time trip back to the glory days of the late 1970s, when I worked on newspapers here and restaurants with equal parts personality and imaginative cuisine were thriving on virtually every block," wrote *New York Times*' Regina Schrambling in 2002. "Those were the wonder years, when people walked to the Frog and the Commissary, to the Astral Plane and Knave of Hearts, to Friday Saturday Sunday. All those were passionate places where the décor might be charmingly improvisational but the food was always both idiosyncratic and polished."

In 2007, I entered the offices of *Philadelphia City Paper*, a fresh-faced college senior trying to leave my written mark on my hometown. Then there was only an intern spot open in the food department, which was a blessing in disguise. I may have known little about the food industry of the city, but I was open to the challenge, to understand what made Philadelphia food lovers tick. This was during the height of food blogging and celebrity chefs. Soon would come Instagram and dinners where no one could eat until all dishes were first photographed on their phones. But there were many incredible restaurants and chefs that made their mark on our dear city well before I dipped my toe into the scene in 2007, and those chefs helped train and shape those who are now the all-stars of our city.

In the pages ahead, I take a century-long journey down memory lane to pay respect to the celebrated restaurants that once were, get to know unforgettable chef personalities that influenced those to come and share treasured recipes that must be remembered long past the days they flew out of restaurant kitchens.

PART I

PHILADELPHIA'S FINE DINING AT ITS FINEST

1
Déjà Vu

1609 Pine Street

How Salomon Montezinos came to Philadelphia to open Déjà Vu is a story within itself. He came from Holland, and after stints in the Netherlands and Switzerland beginning at the ripe age of seventeen as a cook, maître d', waiter and steward, he ended up cooking in Paris in the 1960s. There he met Peter von Starck, who owned La Panetière in Philadelphia. Montezinos wanted to come to America because he believed that in Europe people knew how to cook, and in America, "they had hamburgers." Von Starck hired Montezinos, and during Montezinos's break from La Panetière for his wedding and long honeymoon in Europe, he was encouraged to come back to Philadelphia to open a restaurant of his own.

That restaurant was Déjà Vu. Montezinos was convinced that the United States was the right place for him to locate a restaurant of his own. "America is a growing country and Americans are becoming increasingly interested in gastronomy—plus the fine wines that go with good food," he told the *News Journal* in 1975.

Déjà Vu was located in a 160-year-old private house. After you climbed the steps and passed through the front door, you were acquainted with a ten-table, thirty-two-seat dining room surrounded by baroque luxury you'd expect at Palace of Versailles—let alone in Philadelphia—like hand-painted ceilings and walls, pink satin–lined chairs that matched pink linen tablecloths, billowing damask drapes on tall windows, crystal chandeliers and silver candelabras.

Déjà Vu wasn't always the sheer shine of décor elegance. It started off as a bare-bones bistro, transforming into a brown-walled watering hole elaborately draped and wonderfully Victorian, to its luxe conception driven by elaborate ceiling and floral wall coverings hand-painted by a Florida artist and his team of fifteen in 1977 to match the site's specially woven rug. The walls, made to look like watered silk, were styled as Baroque-Rococo. It quickly transitioned to a prix fixe restaurant, seated more guests and offered five courses for thirty dollars. There was also a private dining room for ten one level down.

Déjà Vu was one of the most expensive restaurants on the East Coast in the mid-70s, known for its "most extravagantly prepared, imaginative cuisine to be found anywhere." (The *Inquirer* reported that it actually took "two men, two weeks and lots of wine to dig out" the space. Four people could dine in complete privacy on a ten-course dinner for $100 a person plus the wine, none of which cost less than $60 a bottle.) Montezinos was experimental in the kitchen, rarely serving the same dish twice. The one important criticism that he had received was that due to his constant need for reinvention, he maybe didn't leave a good thing alone.

"This is one of the best restaurants I have seen in my life," proclaimed notable Louis Szathmary, owner of Chicago's The Bakery, known TV personality and cookbook author. "It is one thing to have imagination; it is another to bring that imagination from the kitchen to the table with such success."

"Déjà Vu is one of the most elegant, gracious little restaurants in town," reported the *Philadelphia Inquirer*'s food editor, Bill Collins, in 1975. "It is also one of the most interesting, if not downright controversial." (Controversial in that, as he wrote, some found his "fancy food sometimes end[ed] in crash landings, and that his prices—dinner for two in the '70s to exceed much more than $50—irrational. Others said the prices were warranted due to the chef using the finest, rare and costly ingredients.") Collins also wrote, "Dining at Déjà Vu is an adventure, often a glorious one."

It was small, highly personal, with a distinctive style of cooking, light and deceptively simple. The cuisine was somewhere between classical French and nouvelle. It was what Collins billed "cuisine Montez." All of the ingredients were naturally grown. Déjà Vu never used white sugar, bleached flour or additives. The eggs were fertilized and farm fresh. Fruits and vegetables were flown in from San Diego. Déjà Vu even installed a soft-treated purified water system, which enhanced the purity and flavor of drinks and food.

"We can't afford organic meats," Montezinos said, "but our fruits and vegetables are organic."

Montezinos became known as the "flying Dutchman of Philadelphia gastronomy" and featured menus based on his travels and his dreams of gastronomic glory. He'd frequently travel back to Paris with his wife, scouting out new French products in the capital and seeking new wine vintages to add to his collection. He proclaimed that he had the "most valuable [wine] cellar on the East Coast," and some of his Madeira wines were as old as vintages from 1826 and 1837. He also had magnums of Mouton Rothschild from its 1947 vintage—priced at the restaurant for purchase of $600.

A dining experience would have potentially included a round of *moules a l'escargot*, ranked as the best served in Philadelphia; an onion soup almost thick enough to eat with chopsticks; *rognons de veau* (veal kidneys in a light whiskey sauce); and poulet curry, stewed with bananas, figs and almonds.

Memorable dishes included the veal liver with caramelized onion, bacon and pinot noir sauce, and the Le Tournedos "Café de Paris," a prime filet with a sauce concocted of twenty-four herbs and spices that was dark, thick and extremely savory.

Aside from the French-inspired dishes, the chef expanded offerings when inspired by other regions. He'd do an Indonesian rice table, a feat only available for a party of ten or more due to the work and preparation involved.

Déjà Vu was important to Philadelphia because it helped usher in the Philadelphia restaurant renaissance in the '70s. In the same league with Le Bec-Fin, La Panetière and La Truffe, it was a sumptuous go-for-baroque experience, a place where romantics lapped up Montezinos's escargot, veal livers and wild duck—creative, ahead of their time, melding of Asian and European dishes enriched by pan reductions and not by gobs of added fat.

"I've always been five years in advance," Montezinos once said. "What I'm doing is good for them. It doesn't make them fat and it isn't too rich."

At the height of Déjà Vu's acclaim, Sal Montezinos's wife, Susan, suggested that "Philadelphia is catching up. The younger generation didn't like the stodginess of the Main Line. Philadelphia was strait-laced and puritanical when I was growing up. Now everyone is coming back to the city."

During its long run, Déjà Vu was ranked by *USA Today* as one of the nation's top sixteen dining spots. *Family Circle* magazine gave praise to Déjà Vu in a 1981 issue for its desserts, spotlighting in particular the decadent frozen chocolate soufflé.

Seeking "warmth and sanity" in 1989, Salomon sold Déjà Vu after fifteen years, and he and his wife left for down south, going on to open two successful restaurants in Palm Beach and Orlando, Florida. He became restaurateur Nicholas Nickolas's corporate and executive chef, jetting across the globe for Nickolas's restaurants in Florida, Illinois and Hawaii. In 1997, Montezinos did resurface in Philadelphia, acting as executive chef of Nickolas's Rittenhouse Hotel.

Déjà Vu Recipe: Barbecued Cornish Hens
Originally published in the *Daily Register*, 1982

The night before, split 4 fresh Cornish game hens down the backbone, but do not separate.

Marinade
¼ cup cold-pressed almond oil (tasteless)
1 clove garlic
1 teaspoon ginger
1 tablespoon peppercorns
1 sprig fresh thyme
3 bay leaves
1 tablespoon raw honey

Heat the oil and add the remaining ingredients. Take from stove and let cool. Roll hens in mixture. Wrap hens in foil and leave in cool place overnight (16 hours for best results). The next day, prepare the sauce.

Sauce
½ cup clarified butter
2 teaspoons curry powder
2 medium-sized shallots, chopped
½ teaspoon cut ginger root
1 cup white wine
2 tablespoons raw orange blossom honey
1 tablespoon mango chutney
2 big coconuts (juice only) or 1 small can coconut juice

Heat butter in medium pan until light brown. Add the curry powder, shallots and ginger root. Add the wine, turn flame up and flame the base. Extinguish.

With a whisk, beat the honey and chutney through mixture. Add the coconut juice and bring to a boil. Cover and simmer for 10 minutes.

Put mixture through a fine colander and heat until desired consistency. (For a stronger sauce, add hot pepper or hot spices. For a thicker sauce, add arrowroot or cornstarch.)

Take hens from marinade, shake off excess oil and barbecue on charcoal grill. While hens are barbecuing, prepare garnish.

Garnish
2 ripe bananas
½ cup flour
2 tablespoons clarified butter
3 tablespoons cold-pressed almond oil
2 large ripe pineapples
2 egg yolks, beaten

Cut bananas in half horizontally. Dust with flour and sauté in pan with butter and oil until light brown.

Cut 4 slices of pineapple about 1½ inches thick, combine with bananas and turn in beaten egg yolks. Fry until golden.

Place barbecued Cornish hems on plate and cover with sauce. Place banana on one side of plate and pineapple on the other. Serve.

2
Deux Cheminees

Originally at 251 South Camac Street, Relocated to 1221 Locust Street

In 2007, after twenty-seven years of service, Fritz Blank, founding chef–proprietor of Deux Cheminees, announced that he was retiring to Thailand, where his partner Leonard Bucki had lived. The legendary French restaurant in Center City on South Camac Street opened in 1979. Named in French after "two chimneys," the city institution, which eventually moved to Twelfth and Locust Streets, built its reputation for serving upscale French cuisine in an intimate fireplace-festooned environment. Previously, Blank was a chief microbiologist at Crozer-Chester Medical Center until he decided to dip his toe into the restaurant industry.

At Deux Cheminees, time was suspended inside this splendidly dressed dining room. Blank celebrated classic technique and fine dining with the utmost care. Every table was dressed with formal place settings, and its décor was coined "early Philadelphia" by *Inquirer* columnist Elaine Tait. Through the years, most of its menu endured, including Blank's signature rack of lamb, sweetbreads, calf's liver in raspberry-vinegar sauce and, the most iconic, Johnnie Walker Red–fortified jumbo lump crab soup—which only went off-menu during "storms at sea."

Three- to four-course prix fixe dinners danced with house-made duck liver pâté, veal sweetbreads with white wine sauce and two impeccable salads. There were chilled grapes steeped in cinnamon-scented burgundy and port that were served as an intermezzo course. Main course showstoppers included seared venison and striped bass fillets. Desserts were just as incredible, including a soulful rendition of fig bread pudding crafted from dried figs he had marinated for two years, frozen Grand Marnier soufflé and a chocolate crepe wrapped around house-made espresso ice cream that, for years, left a sweet impression.

Blank was a stickler for proper salting; he even used a small amount of salt in his sweet whipped cream to stabilize it. He legendarily would sample every batch of soup and sauce in his kitchen from a teacup saucer.

In 1987, Deux Cheminees experienced a devastating fire. It reopened on Locust Street in two adjoining nineteenth-century townhomes designed by Frank Furness. Guests were seated in one of five dining rooms, making it feel like an exclusive—albeit large—dinner party. One of the dining rooms was in the chef's library, and it featured all the appropriate trimmings: a grandfather clock, burgundy curtains and, of course, bookcases lining the walls with the chef's very own collection of French and Italian cookbooks, hundreds of issues of *Gourmet* magazine—some dating to 1943—plus so much more.

Then *Inquirer* columnist Rick Nichols wrote of "Chef Fritz" in 2007 that "his polymathic interests, culinary memory, and spirit of intellectual adventure are irresistible: One moment he deconstructs the duck-liver pâté we're tasting.…The next, he holds forth on the distinctions between workaday caraway seed and charnushka, its black Russian cousin, typically used in flavoring Armenian string cheese."

In an earlier column in 2004, Nichols wrote in relation to Deux Cheminees that "a quarter-century is a stern test for a restaurant. As a measure, come back in 25 years and see how many trendy Stephen Starr enterprises are still on the scene. It's even more of a measure of the man behind the stove."

Blank was deeply invested in history and the food culture, so much so he became known for hosting elaborate re-creations, such as a seventeenth-century English banquet in 1994 to celebrate the Feast of St. Cecilia or his dinner that highlighted the progression of game cookery through the nineteenth century, in 1995. He also once featured an elaborate salad at the Philadelphia Flower Show in 1998 inspired by a seventeenth-century cookbook, *Grande Salat*, including edible flowers and rose petals in the salad's bed of greens. He was often quoted and referenced for his historical food knowledge and investment in the Philadelphia food scene. He'd be quick to talk about snapper soup his grandmother made in Pennsauken in the '50s or about the history of pepper pot soup (similar to New Orleans gumbo) or the origins of scrapple.

Blank even taught at the Restaurant School of Philadelphia and penned papers for Oxford University's food and cookery symposium in the '90s. Papers included deep dives into America's pioneering "cereal kings" and Philadelphia's colonial-era Caribbean flavor.

Prior to moving overseas, Blank donated more than fifteen thousand cookbooks—some of which were scholarly works, some folklore cookery— to the Rare Book & Manuscript Library of the University of Pennsylvania. In 2002, Penn displayed the collection at an exhibit titled *A Chef & His Library*. In 2005, the school also acquired his eccentric assortment of roughly three thousand recipe pamphlets, such as those that come with a Cuisinart appliance.

In September 2014, then in his seventies, Blank said his farewell. True to the nature of retiring to Thailand, he died in Bang Saray.

Deux Cheminees Recipe: Scallops in Gin Cream
Makes 4 servings

1 ¼ pounds bay scallops
Flour
2 tablespoons butter
1 tablespoon peanut oil
4 mushrooms, quartered
1 tablespoon finely chopped garlic
1 teaspoon chopped fresh parsley
2 teaspoons chopped fresh tarragon (or 1 teaspoon dried)
2 teaspoons fresh lemon juice
¼ cup gin
1 ½ cups heavy cream
Salt, pepper

Dust scallops with flour. Heat butter and oil in a large sauté pan over high heat. Add the mushrooms and scallops. Sauté stirring, until scallops are just cooked and light tan, about two minutes. Be careful not to overcook. Remove scallops and mushrooms to platter. Discard the fat in pan.

Add garlic, parsley, tarragon, lemon juice and gin. Return pan to stove and flambé. Be careful; gin throws a large flame. After the flame dies, add the heavy cream and reduce, stirring with a wooden spatula, until the sauce thickens (to coat a spoon). Season with salt and pepper.

Return scallops and mushrooms to the sauce and heat for about one minute. Serve hot in small copper au gratin pans or scallop shells garnished with lemon slices and a spring of parsley.

3
Le Bec-Fin

Originally at 1312 Spruce Street, Relocated to 1523 Walnut Street

Since the early '70s, Philadelphia's culinary scene has changed spectacularly. During that time, nearly four hundred better restaurants opened in Center City, transforming it from a stodgy restaurant town into one offering variety, quality and excitement. But it was 1967 that this transformation began, when French chef Georges Perrier arrived in Philadelphia.

As he told the *New York Times*, "As far as I know, there was no restaurant scene. When I arrived in Philadelphia, this was not much of a restaurant town. It took the French 200 years to do what we have done in 25. In America, people decided to do something, they go to the bottom of things and study well. I think we have to study our art. It's not a birthright."

Prior to opening what the *New York Times*'s Craig Clairborne wrote was "one of the chief glories of French cooking, not only in Philadelphia, but in all of America," Perrier first worked for Peter von Starck at La Panetière, one of Philadelphia's first examples of haute fine dining. The two chefs had previously worked with each other in the beautiful hotel-restaurant Baumanière les Baux de Provence, and von Starck had to have Perrier in his American kitchen.

Von Starck convinced a then twenty-one-year-old Perrier to relocate from Lyons, France, to Philly to run his kitchen. Eventually, von Starck wanted to move his restaurant to a larger space, and that's where Georges stayed behind—in the same space as La Panetière, to make it his own.

Georges Perrier's Le Bec-Fin was—and continues to go down in history as—Philadelphia's most elegant restaurant. *Courtesy of Mike Persico.*

In 1970, Perrier opened his opulent ten-table jewel box of a restaurant off Rittenhouse Square and astutely named it Le Bec-Fin, a French expression that literally translates as "fine beak" but also means "fine palate."

In its infancy, meals would start at eighteen dollars a person, a price that Perrier called a "gourmet bargain." Though as the *Inquirer*'s critic Elaine Tait would suggest in 1973, "That's more than most of us could comfortably spend…what many home cooks consider a week's budget." Yet Perrier thought it was "too little. For what he served, the price was a 'bargain.'"

He quickly seduced the city with his Francophile establishment and, more important, tutored them in Gallic gastronomy like a stern, but conditionally charming headmaster. For almost forty years, Le Bec-Fin was considered the best restaurant in Philadelphia, one of the finest French tables in the United States and a benchmark of rarefied excellence.

Whereas other restaurants would shove diners out the door in an hour, Le Bec-Fin expected no more than two seatings a night.

"Georges was a pioneer in bringing fine dining not just to Philadelphia, but to the United States as well," acclaimed chef Éric Ripert told *Saveur*. "He is the equivalent of Paul Bocuse in America. Tradition and service were always the backbone of Le Bec-Fin. But Georges was always evolving, and there's no doubt his personality was in every plate."

Le Bec-Fin quickly became known as one of the most elegant dining rooms in the country, lined with white damask tablecloths, silver service places, Christofle flatware, Baccarat crystal and Ginori china. Fresh flowers were always on the table. The interior was said to be "like a Fragonard painting" by many.

"Le Bec-Fin was a refuge from the world and the rest of Philadelphia," Philadelphia food critic Craig LaBan told *Saveur*. "It was such a rarefied thing to walk in off Walnut Street into the cloistered entrance way. You'd open the door to find a fantasy world of fabric walls and gilded accents. It was so pure and heightened and refined and you realized the work in haute cuisine had a higher purpose. At Le Bec-Fin, you understood that."

"He created a market for better food and better chefs," another Philadelphia food writer, Michael Klein, said to *Saveur*. "Eating at Le Bec-Fin was a little vacation, and walking into the restaurant was like walking into a Faberge egg. There was a grandeur that made you instantly aware that you were somewhere special. If it was your first time, you were awe struck and dumbfounded. The anticipation was completely real."

Le Bec-Fin was of a different time. It was about bringing the best of France to people in the States, to Philadelphia, and Georges was one of the chefs establishing the real French standard in America. Not everyone could take a trip to France, but Georges was giving you a free trip to Lyons. There were many years, almost two decades, when Le Bec-Fin was among the top ten restaurants in the country.

In 1983, he moved Le Bec-Fin to more grandiose digs on Walnut Street. At first, his elite clientele was shocked by the sight of prostitutes outside his new block. But Perrier put fear into then mayor W. Wilson Goode to clean up the block, and it quickly became known as Philadelphia's Restaurant Row. (Susanna Foo also called it home.)

Meals danced with terrine de legumes foie gras, dressed with embellishments of what the *Inquirer*'s Elaine Tait described as "pencil-slim asparagus, quill-slim haricots verts and a sliver of black truffle, big enough to crunch and be counted." Sweetbreads were sliced thinly and served with "caviar-pearled" quail eggs and hearts of palm. *La tresse de sole* (salmon and Dover sole) was layered into spinach pasta and an orange- and saffron-scented beurre blanc, which to Tait was "a happy *ménage a trois*."

Dessert was an "overeater's dream," with meringue tortes layered with chocolate buttercream, green plum tarts and currant and lemon sorbets.

Tait suggested at the time of her December 1983 review that, with over a decade of experience with Le Bec-Fin, many diners "expect perfection in every detail" from the elite restaurant.

Perrier was notoriously particular, to put it mildly. Stories of his kitchen tantrums were legendary. If something sucked, he told you. If something was good, eventually, he would tell you. Legend Jacques Pépin would stop into Le Bec-Fin when in Philadelphia and once said that Perrier ran his kitchen like a drill sergeant. "Autocratic, disciplined and exacting are the words that come to mind," he said.

You heard his passion almost every night whenever the kitchen door was open. You'd hear profanity and yelling in the dining room. At any other restaurant you say, "What's going on?" At Le Bec-Fin, you just said, "Georges is working tonight."

What was the chef's secret? "His intense regard for details, from the décor and wine glasses to those extraordinary desserts," said John Mariani, the *Esquire* critic who followed Perrier's career. "He is a gastronomic anchor and the culinary inspiration for them all."

As success spawned offshoots, in 1997, Perrier opened his second restaurant, Brasserie Perrier. It was a more relaxed, less expensive alternative to Le Bec-Fin at Sixteenth and Walnut Streets. In 2000, he opened Le Mas Perrier, inspired by the Provençal restaurant where he trained as a young apprentice. By 2012, he had a Main Line baking company, Art of Bread; a Wayne restaurant, Georges; shares of Table 31 in the Comcast Center; and Mia, in Atlantic City.

As Perrier continued to expand his empire, Le Bec-Fin continued to nab national acclaim. In 2000, Le Bec-Fin garnered "America's Best Restaurant" from *Wine Spectator* and "Best Restaurant" from *Food & Wine*. However oddly, in the same year, Mobil Guide dropped the restaurant's rating from five to four stars. Perrier held the five-star rating for eighteen years.

And he fought back. "We changed everything—the manager, the carpet, the décor, the menu, the candlesticks," he told a *Courier Post* reporter. (History be told, Perrier won his star back two years later.)

In 2002, a *Philadelphia Inquirer* critic relayed that "the tired, salmon-colored Louis XVI décor has been replaced by a 19th-century-style Parisian salon replete with gilt molding, woven gold silk panels, and antique mirrors that lend the room the luster of a treasure chest."

Then in 2008, Bec-Fin struggled to remain relevant. The look changed again. As a plea for reinvention, it dialed down its stiff dress code and moved to an à la carte menu. In 2010, Perrier announced his intention to close the restaurant by 2011. The announcement made headlines, splashed with the asking price for the building of $3.9 million and the business for $600,000. Due to a public outcry of those in favor of him staying, he withdrew his listing. And to reinvent, he transformed Le Bec-Fin's downstairs bar to Tryst.

By 2012, Perrier was back to the notion of selling and did so to dapper forty-year-old Nicolas Fanucci, a former Bec-Fin manager who had just spent six years at California's French Laundry. Perrier, of course, concluded his Le Bec-Fin chapter in true Georges fashion, hosting a last dinner in

March 2012 and making a speech that it "should not be a sad night" and he had "absolutely no regrets."

He was sixty-eight years old then and tired. A month prior, the *Philadelphia Inquirer*'s Craig LaBan published a stinging review, snatching away two of the four bells Le Bec-Fin previously earned. As LaBan wrote in the review: "Changing tastes, a fumbling economy, rising competition, and an even more inflated ego (Perrier's) have all played a role in the demise of what was the premier showpiece of Philadelphia dining for an incredible four decades."

During the "last dinner," guests shared their stories, including those of eating at Le Bec-Fin for the first time as children, as cash-starved law students, as corporate strivers and saving the menus as mementos. Many suggested it was Perrier who taught them to appreciate food. There were even guests who flew up from down south for the farewell, not wanting to believe it to be true.

"He outlasted almost all of his four-star French peers," said *Food & Wine*'s Dana Cowin to the *New York Times*. "And I think part of that was because he was so determined and he wanted to evolve."

Many notable Philadelphia chefs got their start in his kitchen, from *Top Chef* winners Nicholas Elmi and Kevin Sbraga to Chip Roman, Daniel Stern, Aliza Green, Michael Schulson, Francesco Martorella, Chris Scarduzio, Lee Styer and Peter Gilmore, among others.

After closing for a renovation, the storied dining room reopened in June with the chef Walter Abrams, also a French Laundry alum, in the kitchen.

The Bec-Fin reboot was said to be "excellent but rather puzzling"; what characterized this restaurant in its prime was no longer in vogue, and Americans were less interested in dining in mini-Versailles grandeur and experiencing fussy French service. Le Bec-Fin 2.0 lasted one year, closing in June 2013, making way for Michelin-starred chef Justin Bogle, who entirely reconverted the space. Bogle opened Avance in December 2013, and though it was never a Le Bec-Fin, it was ambitious.

"We're trying to get as far away from Le Bec-Fin as possible, and not for any other reason than that we're doing our own thing," Bogle told *Philly Eater* prior to opening. "[This] was his restaurant, Georges Perrier's restaurant. It even got a second chance and that didn't work out. This is completely different. And we can't wait to show it all to Philadelphia."

As of June 2013, Perrier had lost ownership of the building in a sheriff's sale, and Avance had to go by October. Painful for many, Le Bec-Fin's acclaimed bricks were transformed into a showroom for Warby Parker, a Philly-bred glasses' startup, as it transitioned into brick-and-mortar retail.

Le Bec-Fin Recipe: Galette de Crabe Le Bec-Fin
Adapted from *Le Bec-Fin Recipes* (Running Press, 1997)
Makes 8 to 10 servings

14 ounces large shrimp, peeled and deveined
1 bunch scallions, sliced into thin rings
3 tablespoons butter
2 whole eggs, cold
2 cups heavy cream, icy cold
2 tablespoons Dijon mustard
1 tablespoon Worcestershire
1 tablespoon Tabasco
1 pound jumbo lump crabmeat, picked clean
2 tablespoons olive oil

Sauce
1 egg yolk
1 tablespoon sherry vinegar
2 tablespoons Dijon mustard
½ cup chicken broth
1 ½ cups olive oil
2 tablespoons whole-grain mustard
Salt, white pepper

Chill shrimp along with the bowl and blade of a food processor in the freezer for 30 minutes. Sauté scallions in 1 tablespoon butter until wilted. Set aside to cool.

Place shrimp in the processor and puree on high speed for 1 minute or until smooth and shiny. Using a rubber spatula, scrape down the side of the bowl; add eggs. Process again until the mixture is smooth and shiny, about 2 minutes. Scrape the bowl. With machine running, slowly pour in the heavy cream. Scrape the bowl and process to make sure the cream is completely incorporated. Remove mixture and place in a bowl. Stir in the mustard, Worcestershire and Tabasco, then gently fold in the cooled scallions and crabmeat.

Place four or five 3-inch oiled ring molds in a lightly oiled nonstick pan. Fill each mold with the mixture, smoothing the tops with a spoon.

Over medium heat, cook the crab cakes until golden brown, about 2 minutes on each side. Once the cakes have browned, push down on the ring molds to cut off any excess crab mixture and remove the rings from around the cakes. Remove crab cakes from the pan. Repeat procedure until all of the crab mixture has been cooked. (The cakes may be made up to 1 day ahead, up to this point, and refrigerated.)

For the sauce, place egg yolk, vinegar, Dijon mustard and chicken broth into a blender. Blend until smooth, about 30 seconds. Drizzle in the olive oil until the sauce is creamy looking. Add the whole-grain mustard and season with salt and pepper to taste.

Preheat oven to 400 degrees. Place crab cakes on a buttered nonstick baking pan. Bake for 5 minutes or until the cakes are springy to the touch. In a small pot, slowly heat the sauce over low heat without letting it boil. Place 1 or 2 crab cakes on a plate and then ladle the sauce over top and serve immediately.

4
Frog, Frog Commissary

FROG 1.0: 1973–1980

In 1964, Steven Poses came to Philadelphia from Yonkers, New York, to study at University of Pennsylvania. After graduation, he trained for the Peace Corps but quit to work with SANE (the Committee for Sane Nuclear Policy). To avoid going to Vietnam, he needed a draft-deferring job and became the media instructor at the private Germantown-based Green Tea School. There, Poses led his students at his first restaurant. "Two days a week, the kids cooked and prepared lunch for the staff," said Poses to the *Philadelphia Inquirer*. "The staff would buy lunch, just like a real restaurant."

Fast forward to 1971, Steven Poses started out working as a busboy, learning how a real restaurant worked and sweeping crumbs off white linen tablecloths. Later he became a chef at La Panetiére around the same time that George Perrier was running the kitchen. This is a testament to Philadelphia—it's a big city with a small-town mentality. Everyone has worked with *someone* at one point in time.

But Steven Poses was meant for other, less fussy things. He decided to strike out on his own, and with $35,000 collected from friends and family, he opened his first fifty-five-seat restaurant, Frog, on North Twentieth Street. In a playful spoof of Manhattan's La Grenouille, Poses called his restaurant "Frög." The umlaut (dots over the *o*) had nothing to do with pronunciation but rather represented the eyes of an imaginary Kermit-like amphibian that became the restaurant's trademark.

Poses may have not cooked like Georges Perrier, but his first, second and third restaurants helped change the way the city ate. He succeeded because of his very '60s attitude and naivety. Steven Poses was, arguably, Philly's first hipster, influenced in equal measure by Julia Child's *Mastering the Art of French Cooking* and Jane Jacobs's *The Death and Life of Great American Cities.*

"What first attracted me to restaurants," Poses said, "was the role that they play in the life of a city. One of the books that had the greatest impact on me in college at Penn was Jane Jacobs's book, 'Death and Life of Great American Cities.' She talks about the importance of a neighborhood candy store as giving people in an otherwise impersonal city a chance to come together. And for me, that was the image of a restaurant."

In 1986, Poses relayed to the *New York Times* that Philadelphia wasn't a trendy town. "What we have is a continued evolution in cuisine." He related the city to his scaled-down menu that blended American, Asian and French cooking. He broke new culinary ground in a traditionally meat-and-potatoes town, a hit with young adult singles of Poses's generation who, like him, flocked to downtown townhouses in search of the good life. He wanted it to be a comfortable neighborhood establishment where people could come together, enjoy good food and discuss the issues of the day.

And the Frog succeeded at that. Steven Poses's places weren't the first of their kind, but they were the best and most revered among similar contemporaries like the Black Banana, Lickety Split and Astral Plane. Before their appearance, informal dining in America (not just Philly) was rarely desirable and never chic.

His restaurant was notoriously informal, with bright green splashed around, laden with spider plants, mismatched chairs (including pews) and frog paraphernalia. "I vividly recall the evening a longhaired blonde waitress took a seat at our table and asked what we'd like to eat," wrote Alan Richman, food critic for the *Broad Street Review*. "That was heart-pounding intimacy back then. That was the Frog in 1973."

Frog was an absolute game changer, forever shifting the trajectory of Philadelphia dining. It's hard to believe now, but going out for dinner in Philadelphia in the early '70s was a stuffy affair. Everything came under the stiff rubric of fine dining, with tuxedoed waiters serving leathery steak and canned peas to sharply dressed diners. "Into that milieu strode an artist in chef whites, a Peace Corps trainee-turned-antiwar protestor who wondered why food couldn't be *the* thing to bring people together in the big, cold city," wrote the *New York Times*. That was Poses.

But in his kitchens, he made his mark by bringing together international flavors in a time before the term *fusion* had any culinary connotations. Frog and its casual counterpart, the Commissary, were expanding palates throughout the region with international flavors. Poses brought colleague Kamol Phutlek to the Frog and gave Philadelphia a glimpse of early Asian fusion cooking. Poses doesn't claim great culinary inspiration from one of, if not the, city's most acclaimed chefs. He's pulled inspiration from the people he's worked with, people with parents from Italy, China, Ireland, Thailand, Japan and Iran.

"Running a restaurant is a team sport," said Poses. "You can't run a restaurant without a team of people who share your passion. Ultimately, they're like your children. They grow up, move on and leave the nest." A year after opening, he took over the apartment behind the Frog and expanded his restaurant to nearly ninety seats.

FROG COMMISSARY: 1977–1991

Philadelphia food writer Holly Moore once wrote, "The Commissary convinced me that W.C. Fields had it wrong."

Poses introduced the Commissary in 1977, and it featured a menu today's food lovers would gush over in a cafeteria setting. It was arguably Philadelphia's first gourmet cafeteria, still seen as having been one of the best. (Imagine it as an '80s version of Eataly, minus the heavy Italian influences.) There was sushi before anyone knew it was cool and communal dining tables long before the phrase entered anyone's lexicon. It was a place where Philadelphians would go to escape big-city isolation. "We're all in this together," Poses would think, gazing with pride on students breaking bread alongside lawyers and blue-collar workers.

The original Commissary concept was to dish out caviar-class food in a chic cafeteria setting. Later, for the fans of Commissary food who would rather sit and be served, Poses added a small, full-service dining room upstairs known as, you betcha, "Upstairs at the Commissary." The Commissary owes its success to convenience as well as its unusual food combinations.

Doors opened early to pamper the breakfasting crowd with fresh-baked croissants and well-made omelets. After that, there was all-day service on salads, charcuterie and a bevy of hot specials. For the upstairs diner, the big blackboard chalked up an even more imaginative menu.

Lunch would start with something like cold gazpacho and then move on to something more exotic such as batter-fried sole with bananas or chicken fruit salad with horseradish mayonnaise. Dinner would begin with grilled oysters and anchovy butter; followed by a Thai beef curry with cashews, oranges and snow peas; and then finish with chocolate mousse cake or Sachertorte—both first-rate creations from the Commissary's staff of bakers.

"I worked at the Commissary during the summers when I was in college, and I still remember the [strawberry heart tart] recipe," said Alison Barshak, chef/owner of Alison Two. "The tarts were beautiful, but they didn't last overnight, so at the end of the night we could eat any leftovers."

In 1985, Poses was on a mission to redo the design of Commissary to make it as much of a breakthrough as it was the year it opened, with the intent to keep it fun.

The Commissary earned him a spot in the first 50 Who's Who of Cooking in America, alphabetically nestled between Robert Mondavi and Paul Prudhomme.

FROG 2.0: 1980–1987

After several successful years of serving imaginative food in a friendly, noisy storefront, Frog hopped around the corner to a bigger, grander brownstone on Locust Street in December 1980. "The 'new' Frog was grown-up, contemporary, understated and spacious—in short, everything the old Frog was not," wrote *Philadelphia Inquirer* critic Elaine Tait. "There was a piano bar downstairs, at basement level. There was another room above the kitchen in the back."

The menu included notorious favorites from the original Sixteenth Street location, plus a variety of new dishes that were changed with the season. Dishes most intriguing for the time were the filet mignon with snails and garlic herb butter; grilled, marinated vegetables with tofu; and baked snails in pasta shells with spinach, garlic, walnuts and Pernod.

By 1984, Poses had many additional offshoots, including the Piano Bar at the Commissary and the Market, a gourmet to-go emporium around the corner from the Commissary; Eden cafeterias; 16th Street Bar & Grill, a storefront restaurant in the original Frog location; City Bites, a restaurant inspired by trendy LA in Society Hill catering to "new wave theater"; USA Café, a transformation of the Upstairs at the Commissary with Southwest cuisine; and a catering service—which still operates today.

By 1984, Poses's restaurants were bringing in $11 million a year, employing five hundred people and serving four thousand meals daily, and he was dubbed the "Man Who Fathered the Philadelphia Restaurant Renaissance" and—especially at the time—the "Man Who Is Seen a Lot on Seventeenth Street."

"Poses mini-empire had become recognized as an exciting restaurant organization," relayed Paul Roller, a chef at the original Frog and later at Commissary, to the *Philadelphia Inquirer*. "Things were going very well financially. Some of the heavy catering weeks, the business was grossing $100,000. In the early days, the impact was close to awesome." (Roller left the Poses empire in 1982 to open his own namesake restaurant in Chestnut Hill.)

Through his empire's progression, Poses continued to be involved in his restaurants. He'd carry a stack of index cards in his pocket to jot down recipe ideas or reminders of who to call. "Poses talks about being able to 'cook in [his] head,' but sometimes the transmission of concept to conception doesn't work out," reported *Philadelphia Inquirer* on Poses funkier dish concepts, served for the twentieth anniversary gala of the Pennsylvania Ballet. In short, it was a seaweed pasta that was seaweed-flavored pasta made to look like seaweed served atop an artfully arranged seaweed salad. No cliffhanger here—it needed some work.

Along the way, in 1985, he garnered enough buzz for himself and his restaurants that he began publishing his recipes in print, first releasing *The Frog Commissary Cookbook* in partnership with Anne Clark and Becky Roller. He also started an umbrella organization that oversaw his restaurant empire called Shooting Stars Inc. At the time, Poses owned the largest upscale restaurant organization in Philadelphia.

On November 28, 1987, Poses decided to bid farewell to the Frog. The restaurant that weaned Philadelphians off their steak and lobster dinners had been losing money. Some blamed new restaurants in town that took cues from what Poses did best and ultimately stole his business. Others blamed baby boomers for becoming couch potatoes and not dining out as frequently. (Ha.)

On the final day of service, as reported by the *Inquirer*, local Renee Slobasky noted that Poses "was in the forefront of [the] city's restaurant renaissance, and coming [to the Frog] had always been an experience in eating." Poses suggested that closing the Frog was "the right and necessary decision.…Even when you make these mature decisions, growing up is a little hard."

Though he closed the Frog, he continued to operate the Commissary for a few years, until he focused his empire solely on catering, in partnership with the Franklin Institute.

In 2010, Poses made an appearance with Frog Burger, a Franklin Institute lawn project with his son and wife that received its fair share of digital ink in the height of food blogging. During this stint, his infamous carrot cake (recipe to follow) and chocolate fudge "killer cake" reemerged, made famous at his Frog Commissary. They were served in traditional and milkshake forms.

Frog Commissary Recipe: Carrot Cake
Adapted from *The Frog Commissary Cookbook*
(Camino Books Inc., 2002)

Pecan Cream Filling
1 ½ cups sugar
¼ cup flour
¾ teaspoon salt
1 ½ cups heavy cream
6 ounces (¾ cup) unsalted butter
1 ¼ cups chopped pecans
2 teaspoons vanilla extract

Carrot Cake
1 ¼ cups corn oil
2 cups sugar
2 cups flour
2 teaspoons cinnamon
2 teaspoons baking powder
1 teaspoon baking soda
1 teaspoon salt
4 eggs
4 cups grated carrots (about a one-pound bag)
1 cup chopped pecans
1 cup raisins

Cream Cheese Frosting
8 ounces soft unsalted butter
8 ounces soft cream cheese

1-pound box powdered sugar
1 teaspoon vanilla extract
4 ounces (1 ½ cups) shredded, sweetened coconut

Make filling: In a heavy saucepan, blend well the sugar, flour and salt. Gradually stir in cream. Add butter. Cook and stir mixture over low heat until the butter has melted and then let simmer 20–30 minutes until golden brown in color, stirring occasionally. Cool to lukewarm. Stir in the nuts and vanilla. Let cool completely and refrigerate overnight. If too thick to spread, bring to room temperature before using.

Make cake: Preheat oven to 350 degrees. Have ready a greased and floured 10-inch tube cake pan. In a large bowl, whisk together the corn oil and sugar. Sift together the flour, cinnamon, baking powder, baking soda and salt. Sift half the dry ingredients into the sugar-oil mixture and blend. Alternately sift in the rest of the dry ingredients while adding the eggs, one by one. Combine well. Add carrots, raisins and pecans. Pour into the prepared tube pan and bake for 70 minutes. Cool upright in the pan on a cooling rack. If you are not using the cake that day, it can be removed from the pan, wrapped well in plastic wrap and stored at room temperature.

Make frosting: Cream butter well. Add the cream cheese and beat until blended. Sift in the sugar and add the vanilla. If too soft to spread, chill a bit. Refrigerate if not using immediately but bring to a spreadable temperature before using.

Assemble cake: Preheat oven to 300 degrees. Spread coconut on a baking sheet and bake for 10–15 minutes until it colors lightly. Toss the coconut occasionally while it is baking so that it browns evenly. Cool completely. Have the filling and frosting at a spreadable consistency. Loosen the cake in its pan and invert onto a serving plate. With a long, serrated knife, carefully split the cake into 3 horizontal layers. Spread filling between the layers. Spread the frosting over the top and sides. Pat the toasted coconut onto the sides of the cake. If desired, reserve ½ cup of the frosting and color half with green food coloring and half with orange. Then decorate the top of the cake with green and orange icing piped through a 1/16-inch-wide plain pastry tube to resemble little carrots. Serve cake at room temperature.

5

The Fountain at the Four Seasons Hotel

1 Logan Square

On July 31, 1983, one of Philadelphia's most-decorated restaurants, the Fountain, made its debut in the Four Seasons Hotel. That was when Ronald Reagan was in the White House and the Phillies were on their way to the World Series. Chef Jean-Marie Lacroix was at its helm, deep in the white-walled kitchen that would, through its years, shepherd several iconic French chefs into what quickly became one of Philadelphia's most luxurious landmarks.

The Fountain restaurant was the definition of gold-plated elegance, with a location that overlooked the majestic Swann Memorial Fountain sculpture by Alexander Stirling Calder in the center of Logan Square. (Mind you, this sculpture influenced the restaurant's name.) Sitting in the restaurant, you would also be able to enjoy sweeping views of the Benjamin Franklin Parkway, making it one of the most scenic dining destinations in Philadelphia for its time.

The Fountain restaurant was serene with a color scheme of grays, silvers, lavenders, blues and browns. It changed its display of artwork often to add alternating splashes of color to increase eye appeal. The elegant setting hosted all-day dining, from breakfast to lunch and especially dinner.

Chef Jean-Marie Lacroix made his name at the Fountain, cooking there for more than two decades, before moving on to open his namesake restaurant, Lacroix at the Rittenhouse. (During Lacroix's tenure at the Fountain, he won the prestigious James Beard Foundation's Best Chef/Mid-Atlantic award.) Locals also attributed Lacroix with helping shape the high caliber of culinary talent in Philadelphia; many got their start or secured a stint in the Fountain's glamorous kitchen, including chefs like Tony Clark and Bruce Lim.

"The Four Seasons was more accessible to us than Le Bec-Fin," recalled Steven Poses. "It was the beginning of a more professional standard for this city, raising the bar from an era of enthusiastic amateurs. We didn't have the fine linens or fancy silver. But once the Fountain came along there was a sense of 'oh this is what it can be.' It redefined how good you had to be to compete."

There was minimal turnover in the kitchen, including longtime culinary maestro Martin Hamann, who eventually left to work at the equally high-brow Union League after twenty-five years in the kitchen. David Jansen was the dinner chef for twenty-two years during its glory days before he left in 2010. The final Fountain chef, William DiStefano ("Chef Billy," as the staff called him), had been with the hotel for twenty-five years, rising from apprentice to head chef, the last lifer in a long line (after David Jansen and Martin Hamann) to run this thoroughbred kitchen brigade.

DiStefano attributed the success to a menu that changed with the seasons, even as the dining room maintained its posh, white linen sensibility. "That was the reason I think we survived so long," said DiStefano to the *Philadelphia Inquirer*. "We were always looking to adapt. We were always looking to change."

In this kitchen, there were no shortcuts, and the world's best ingredients were limited only by the imagination. Lacroix was instrumental in helping to develop regional sources for meat, produce and breads, and other restaurants quickly followed suit. The kitchen had amazing consistency, which was a tribute to the longevity of its talented stalwarts. Pull all the longtime chefs' experiences, from the day and night chefs, to the chef *tournant*, banquet chef and pastry chef, and you'd have more than a century of Fountain experience among them.

At breakfast, you'd find options like the Fountain Benedict, crafted on a goat cheese biscuit with expertly poached eggs, pancetta and a chive hollandaise; or French toast filled with Nutella. No one did steak and eggs like the Fountain: beef carpaccio topped with Pont Neuf potatoes and a tempura-fried egg yolk that released a brilliant yellow gush at the cut of a fork. Weekend brunch meant the most luxe morning buffet a local could dream of, while at lunch you could consider cauliflower velouté with truffle or French onion soup or roasted chicken breast with risotto or hanger steak with sweet potatoes.

There were classic indulgences that made it easy for splurging diners to enjoy things the "Fountain way," such as dry-aged steak topped with a bundle of baby carrots tied with ramps and a sheer flower made from crisped potato petals—an entrée once called "edible still life" in print. The lobster duo, with a buttery tail and huge sautéed shrimp, crowned a large ravioli filled with lobster, potato and leeks and was seen as the city's "most elegant lobster splurge." The rabbit was transformed three ways: grilled, bones roasted down into champagne-mustard vinaigrette and the legs turned into rich rillettes topped with a *gelée* of orange.

Let us not forgot about dessert with its exquisite delicacies, like apple sticky toffee pudding with cognac ice cream, Meyer lemon tart with blueberry compote or the famous crystal cart with twenty-plus artisan cheeses that would be flipped open for you to explore with your hungry eyes.

Of course, for the truest corporate-card diner, there was a fine list of wines that lay stocked in a vast six-hundred-label cellar.

There were veteran servers too, like Jim Miller and Ron Streicher, who in the elegant wood-paneled restaurant would buff the crystal to a gleam and pampered customers with cheese-cart luxury up until the restaurant's close. They'd polish the silver too—each guest experienced a setting of ten pieces through the course of their meal.

The Fountain would also go to extreme levels to ensure its elegance was the city's—and world's—finest. It installed a filtration system to replace all the expensive bottled European water it used to cook with as a nod as much to economy as to green ecology.

As one of the truest stalwarts of fine dining in Philadelphia, the Fountain held a rare four-bell rating from the *Inquirer*'s Craig LaBan in 2009. This was especially an honor, given it was a period of time in Philadelphia's dining scene where restaurants shifted from jackets-required mentalities to those, as LaBan put it, that "unbuttoned their double-breasted dress codes."

In fact, LaBan's meals at the Fountain were so spectacular that in the age of less-stuffy dining he'd "look forward to another dinner there even if the Fountain required straitjackets and gravity boots."

The Fountain did not just catch LaBan's attention. It achieved ratings from multiple travel guides: five diamonds from AAA—the only restaurant in the region—and *Forbes* Travel Guide Five Star (an ultra-exclusive list of twenty-one five-star restaurants in the United States and Canada, with no other Philadelphia restaurant nabbing the title with the exception of Le Bec-Fin and Lacroix). It repetitively topped the rankings of *Zagat Survey's* thirty-point scale, achieving high ranks across the board for food, décor and service—something that few restaurants in the country have achieved. Buzzy statements like "elegance personified," "perfect attention to detail" and "well taken care of through the whole experience" rang true throughout the survey results.

The Fountain hosted many a corporate titan during its thirty-one-year run. *Philadelphia Inquirer*'s food columnist Michael Klein told *WHYY* in 2014 that its finest attribute was "the staff's willingness to give the same unblinking attention to big shots and common folks alike. It didn't matter if you were a CEO or a working guy who saved up years for this one dinner, they treated everybody equally."

"Owners also had a propensity to hire loyal staff and promote from within," Klein continued.

To modernize in its later years, the historically gouging wine list received slightly lower markups, plus there were sixty wines under $60. There was a new $62 tasting menu on weekdays (versus the more expensive, larger weekend options). And even prices on the à la carte menu, whose entrées once hovered obscenely in the $50-plus range, had been lowered an average of $7 a plate.

After thirty-one years, the Fountain served its final dinner service on Saturday, December 27, 2014. The Four Seasons Hotel, where the restaurant made its home, announced earlier that year in January that it would be leaving its longtime Logan Square location to take up residence in the upper levels of the Comcast Innovation and Technology Center tower at Eighteenth and Arch Streets. (Now, the Four Seasons holds its elite dining experience on its fifty-ninth floor, a namesake restaurant for Michelin-starred chef Jean-Georges.) At the time of the announcement, the Fountain's restaurant management felt it would be more dignified "to give the Fountain its own designated departure time," and that became the end of the year.

In total, the Fountain was proud to serve 11,473 dinners in its three decades of service. Urban Farmer, a high-end steakhouse built around sourcing local, farm-to-table ingredients, took over residence of the storied Fountain location home.

The Fountain Recipe: Roasted Orange Chicken Breast with Wild Rice Pancakes

Adapted from the *Philadelphia Inquirer*, September 2007

½ cup chopped pecans
1 cup chicken stock
1 cup orange juice
Zest of 1 orange

2 tablespoons cornstarch
2 tablespoons water
Coarse salt, freshly ground black pepper, to taste
1 (6.2-ounce) package wild rice mix
2 large eggs, lightly beaten
½ cup bread crumbs
2 tablespoons olive oil
2 tablespoons unsalted butter
4 boneless skinless chicken breast halves
1 (12-ounce) can Mandarin orange segments, drained

Preheat oven to 350 degrees. Place pecans on a sheet pan and bake, stirring once or twice, until they are lightly toasted and fragrant, 3 to 4 minutes. Set aside.

In a small saucepan, combine the chicken stock, orange juice and orange zest. Bring to a boil over high heat, lower the heat and simmer until reduced by half, about 10 minutes.

In a cup, combine the cornstarch and water and stir until smooth. Whisk the cornstarch into the boiling stock and orange juice and cook, stirring, until thickened, about 2 minutes. Season with salt and pepper and set aside.

Meanwhile, prepare wild rice mix according to package directions, transfer to a large bowl and allow to cool slightly. Stir in the eggs and the bread crumbs. Form into 8 pancakes.

In a large sauté pan, combine 1 tablespoon of the olive oil and 1 tablespoon of the butter over medium-high heat. When the butter melts, working in two batches, cook the pancakes until golden on each side, about 4 minutes per batch. Keep warm.

Wipe out the skillet the pancakes cooked in and return it to medium heat. Add the remaining 1 tablespoon olive oil and 1 tablespoon butter. Season the chicken with salt and pepper. Cook the chicken over medium-high heat until the breasts just start to brown and are cooked through, about 10 minutes.

To serve, reheat sauce if necessary. Slice cooked chicken breasts on the bias into six to eight slices each. Place two rice pancakes on each of four plates. Arrange the chicken on the pancakes. Ladle sauce over each serving, place a few mandarin orange segments on each plate and scatter with pecans.

6

The Garden

1617 Spruce Street

Kathleen Mulhern was a Philadelphia entrepreneur who helped spark the city's restaurant renaissance in the spring of 1974 by opening a tiny eatery that quickly became famous as The Garden. Starting just off 1617 Spruce Street, Mulhern, who had no previous experience in running a restaurant, came equipped only with a vision of what she wanted the eatery to be. She started by opening a small storefront named Le Take-Out in her building, which featured refined prepared foods like daily soups, chicken salad and chocolate cake to neighborhood dozens. Quickly, however, a first-floor main dining room was added, then the courtyard seating, and Le Take-Out transformed into what would be known as The Garden.

"After working for years at a number of nondescript, unrewarding jobs, I finally got the courage to go into business for myself," Mulhern reminisced at the height of her restaurant career to the *New York Times*. "I opened a needlepoint shop in the '70s and lucked out, made enough to hire a manager and then decided to open a restaurant! [I was] a very lucky woman: no training, undercapitalized and with no supervisory experience. I was very fortunate to find some talented people who went along with my dream and the rest is history."

Lucky she may have been, but she had an elegant vision, which quickly catapulted into a celebrated, and somewhat expensive, Philadelphia restaurant. Her culinary vision was informed by trips she had taken to Europe, especially Paris, where she enjoyed wonderful meals, took mental notes and then taught herself to cook once she arrived home. She learned culinary skills by "loving to eat and going to France."

Getting financing to start The Garden was not easy, she told the *Inquirer* in 1980. "No one wanted to talk with me," she said. "I embarrassed the hell out of people, but I had this vision."

Mulhern soon learned that she was on to something. People began flocking to The Garden, which expanded and began to draw the city's wealthy and powerful.

It was profoundly dressed in floral wallpaper, lace curtains and soft green carpet. English prints and soft lights hung throughout the dining rooms, and unobtrusive music echoed as the soundtrack, from Aznavour to Sinatra. It was like a private club—Kathleen Mulhern's very own club—where she branded her own attitude of discreet luxury to loyal customers with the aid of coolly professional staff.

"Lots of people had traveled and were aware there was something better out there," she told the *New York Times* in 1986. "Young people were making more money and were interested in dining. A lot of new people were coming into the city. We opened in response to a demand, a change in the city."

When the Philadelphia Orchestra was in town, concerts weren't complete without a meal at The Garden, but that wasn't the only time diners swung by. Lazy summer dinners in the starlit garden of this old brownstone became a Philly thing with the locals who didn't escape to the shore.

Overtime, Mulhern estimated that her four private dining rooms in her charming pair of interconnecting nineteenth-century townhouses accounted for nearly 70 percent of her revenue. (Overall, the restaurant was triumphant, consisting of five separate dining rooms—including the clubby Oyster Bar and rooms named the Swan and the Eagle—as well as two areas of outdoor seating, a deck off of the Small Bar and a garden courtyard.)

Mulhern also benefited from the booming stock market and buoyant economy in the late '70s, which helped explain the rise in reservations for her private dining rooms.

"During Mayor Bill Green's administration, Green and his cabinet would often lunch in the Swan Room, famous for the antique swan decoys," said Harry Adamson, a former waiter at The Garden. "Philadelphia Museum of Art's President Robert Montgomery Scott was at The Garden every day for luncheon at table 28, coming and going from Fairmount on his fold-up bicycle."

By the '80s, Philadelphia columnists like Mike Shoup had begun to take note. "Today, you can dine at The Garden, and it takes no twist of the arm to conclude that it's one of the city's best," he wrote in the *Inquirer*. "My personal feeling is that The Garden and its contemporaries, more than any other factor, are what have given the city its new image and character."

Fans of The Garden claim that you could dine there every day of the week and never become bored or disappointed.

Lunch was a statement of the time, with its delights of glazed baked ham with French mustard; warm, French-style potato salad; and chunky chicken and walnut salad with house-made mayonnaise. The bar featured an interesting selection of aperitifs, including the then fashionable Bocuse creation of white wine and framboise.

Tina Pappajohn, one of Mulhern's assistants for a number of years, said The Garden was "one of the early renaissance restaurants in Philadelphia that changed the whole world."

Mulhern and her staff worked diligently to make the food and dining experience memorable. "All the mirrors and glass sparkled, the copper gleamed, the food was uncommonly beautiful and delicious," Pappajohn said. "Every effort was made to remove every bone from every fish."

Comically, male waiters were said to think Mulhern was a terror at times, but that was because she was a perfectionist. Everything from the food to the wine, flowers, atmosphere, service and waiters' aprons and oxford shirts had to be first-rate. The Garden became like a finishing school for the restaurant business, where the employees could learn about food, fine wine and gracious service.

Through its quarter-century success, The Garden's winning philosophy was "consistency and reliability." There was nothing nouvelle or fusion about Mulhern's approach to food. She simply believed in presenting the best that her purveyors had to offer, prepared lovingly.

The menu had a particular emphasis on raw oysters, filet mignon and Maine lobsters, as well as other straightforward, elegant dishes like smoked salmon, prosciutto on melon, veal chops and roasted rack of lamb. A diner could expect to get an entrée within the range of $19.95 for an old-fashioned roast chicken and garlic mashed potatoes to $29.95 for a sixteen-ounce New York sirloin. The beef carpaccio was silky and notorious, dazzled with particularly piquant capers; thinly sliced calves' livers were expertly flavored, served with roasted shallots and crispy pommes frites. Salads changed daily, with a notable example being one smothered rich Roquefort cheese baked in the lightest and crispiest of phyllo and served over a fresh bed of mixed greens with toasted walnuts and a mustard vinaigrette.

The Garden's wine list featured dependable wines from dependable shippers. You could find a Burgundy from Faiveley or a Sonoma Cutrer Chardonnay by the glass or a bottle of a second-growth Bordeaux that fit your budget. Profiteroles for dessert were almost a given, with a glass of Sauternes that many were still discovering.

"We have a couple of 'dazzle' things on the menu, but quality and consistency are what we strive for," Mulhern relayed confidently in 1986.

In the September 1998 issue of *Bon Appétit* magazine, The Garden was honored as one of the top ten U.S. restaurants that successfully stood the test of time.

Spruce Street's culinary dowager closed after a fire in 2000, just two weeks before Christmas. During the height of Mulhern's acclaim, she did open another restaurant, Harry's Bar and Grill at 22 South Eighteenth Street. It closed in the mid-'90s, which Mulhern described as nearly breaking her heart.

The restaurant renaissance matriarch lived until she was ninety-three years old, remaining actively engaged in Philadelphia's current food scene until she passed in 2018.

The Garden Recipe: Shellfish Fricassee
Adapted from the *Philadelphia Inquirer*, January 1988
Makes 6 servings

1 cup fish stock (recipe to follow)
½ cup crème fraiche
1 tablespoon finely minced garlic
1 teaspoon white pepper
1 tablespoon tomato paste
¼ pound (1 stick) unsalted butter, softened
36 mussels
30 littleneck clams
18 oysters
Finely chopped parsley, for garnish

Combine fish stock, crème fraiche, garlic, pepper and lemon juice. Heat, stirring occasionally until sauce thickens. Add tomato paste. Cut butter into tablespoon-size pieces. Over a low flame, add butter, one piece at a time at first, whisking until the butter blends in. Do not allow to simmer.

While sauce cooks, steam the shellfish. Save juices. After shellfish have opened, remove from steamer. Strain broth and stir a half cup of broth into the sauce.

Arrange six mussels, five clams and three oysters on each serving plate. Spoon hot sauce over shellfish. Garnish with chopped parsley.

The Garden Recipe: Fish Stock
Makes about 2 quarts

5 pounds sole or red snapper bones
½ teaspoon salt
1 teaspoon lemon juice
4 stalks celery
1 onion
½ teaspoon thyme
½ teaspoon black peppercorns
4 bay leaves
1 teaspoon red pepper flakes
⅓ cup white wine
8 parsley stems
3 quarts water

Soak fish bones in a general amount of water, salt and lemon juice for 20 minutes. Rinse, place in stockpot with celery, onion, thyme, peppercorns, bay leaves, red pepper flakes, wine and parsley. Add three quarts of water. Simmer for 30 minutes.

7

Wanamaker's Crystal Tearoom

100 East Penn Square

John Wanamaker opened the country's first department store restaurant in Philadelphia with the Crystal Tearoom—then called the Grand Crystal Tearoom. Opening on April 5, 1911, on the ninth floor, the menu offered caviar with potato puffs, sole marguery, sweetbreads and, appropriately, Philadelphia cream cheese. The twenty-thousand-square-foot room—now a banquet hall—was one of the largest dining rooms in the city and even the country, with seating for 1,500, twenty-one-foot ceilings, great columns of English brown oak and chandeliers. Many children had their first taste of fine dining there. It was a place that became known for its charm, gentility and good food.

The space was so massive that a waitress would need to jaunt several hundred feet to simply fetch a pitcher of water. According to one of the Wanamaker's history books, there was ample equipment for the serving of ten thousand oysters or ovens equipped to roast seventy-five turkeys all at once. It took more than 50 waitresses, each handling only four tables, to fetch orders for approximately 1,500 customers.

The space itself was modeled after the famous tearoom in the house of Robert Morris, the financier of the Revolution.

Robert Montgomery Scott, retired chief executive officer of the Philadelphia Museum of Art, recalled the popular lunch spot in the '50s, when he was practicing law. "The partners would go bore themselves to

Lunch or dine today in our famous Crystal Tearoom!

It's an institution, famous in its own way as our Independence Hall . . . a showplace to which you bring your out-of-town friends . . . a gourmet's delight! And business men tell us we have the best 65c lunch in town! Come in any day . . . luncheons from noon 'til 2:30 p. m. . . . or have dinner with us Wednesday or Friday nights, 5:00 until 8:00 p. m. Lobster a la Newburg with Wild Rice is just one of the delightful dishes to be served tonight. Ninth Floor—Chestnut.

Above: An advertisement from February 1943 promoting lunch and dinner at the Crystal Tearoom. *Courtesy of* Philadelphia Inquirer.

Left: A scene of the Wanamaker's Crystal Tearoom in 1981. *Courtesy of Old Images of Philadelphia.*

death at the Mid-Day Club, and the associates would go to the Crystal Tearoom for BLTs."

An ad in the *Philadelphia Inquirer* from 1943 reads, "Gourmets sigh over our Crab Ravigote with hearts of celery and sliced tomato….Businessmen say ours is the best lunch in town for 65 cents….Little folks love our special children's menus."

The restaurant was open during store hours and served lunches and afternoon tea snacks; on select nights when the store was open late, it would serve dinners as well.

"Are you in a rush?" wrote Elaine Tait, food columnist of the *Inquirer*, in 1972. "The grandmotherly pace of the tearoom waitresses will drive you to distraction so plan to make your visit a leisurely one." A Saturday lunch would come at the expense of nearly two hours of your time.

The Crystal Tearoom changed its paper menu often, reprinting it daily. However, you'd always find the notorious triangular tea sandwiches. The tea sandwiches were so popular that staff joked that if they removed them from the menu, customers would "hang them by Billy Penn's hat."

The strongest thing there was tea that arrived to your table in its own silver teapot.

Desserts were a high point of the meal, with options like biscuit-type strawberry shortcake (in 1972, priced at sixty cents) and meringue glacé.

The Crystal Tearoom has spawned countless family stories and innumerable memories. Alice Kennedy, a hostess who clocked over thirty years from the '50s to '80s, said she had seated the grandchildren of customers she first met when she started to work at the restaurant. It was such a part of folks' lives that parents would come and still be waited on by the same waitress who took their orders as kids.

Ann Pikes worked thirty-four years as a Crystal Tearoom waitress, telling the *Inquirer* in 1982 that it was as much fun then as it was when she started in the '40s. She'd tackle a heavy lunch shift on Black Fridays or clear the decks to wait tables in the evening for handsome cadets who would traditionally dine after the Army-Navy game. "Oh, I remember, we worked like a dog, and we'd love to see all those good-looking young men."

It was always a special place for a grandma to treat her grandchildren, for mother-daughter shopping trips to pause over a platter of tea sandwiches and for ubiquitous, frosted-haired ladies to make their elegant repast during a daily social event.

The Crystal Tearoom was the first of its kind, bringing high-end dining to its high-end department store. In 1982, the store's vice president of food services, John O'Donnell, shared that more and more department stores were discovering that "food is as fashionable as fashion itself," encouraging them to persuade shoppers to not only shop but also eat at their restaurants. This sheer fact alone helped push the Crystal Tearoom to be more competitive against other Center City lunchtime establishments.

In 1995, the Crystal Tearoom restaurant closed to the public. It was then restored as a private banquet hall that could accommodate sit-down receptions up to one thousand people.

In addition to the famous Crystal Tearoom, there was also a balcony café, the Terrace on the Court, on the third floor facing the Grand Court, where shoppers could hear the Wanamaker Organ as they dined. In 2006, Macy's became the occupant of the former Wanamaker Department Store, which is now a National Historic Landmark. In 2008, Macy's closed the Grand Court restaurant.

8
La Truffe

10 South Front Street

La Truffe was the third cozy bistro to grace South Front Street with its presence. First came Janine et Jeannine, then La Boheme, both of which were chic French restaurants that had price tags that outshined the cuisine or service itself.

But in February 1974, the suave Les Smith, an alum of La Panetière and Le Bec-Fin, became a partner with owner and wife Jeannine Mermet. They also brought on twenty-five-year-old Glen John, a promising young chef, to take over the kitchen.

La Truffe was named after the rare and expensive European fungus, the truffle. It was an elegant little French restaurant, perfectly fine and fancy and one of the prettiest in town. Tables was laid with mismatched china and crystal; the dining room was lined with a banquette covered with soft, printed cushions and pillows propped against one wall and a wide-open seating on the others. Mirrors and flocked wallpaper covered the walls, and a pianist played classical music nonstop on Wednesday and Friday nights. To some, it felt like you stepped into a stiff, proper banquet at Versailles.

Upstairs, you'd find a sedate cocktail-and-music lounge that opened only on select nights.

Though with Smith at the helm of Front Street, the prices didn't change. It still cost a couple thirty to fifty dollars for a meal. Prices were so high, though, that some may have needed to find themselves in the kitchen washing dishes at the end of the night. But the food was achievably more acclaimed.

It was a traditional French restaurant where you could enjoy a traditional French multicourse meal: soup, hors d'oeuvres, fish, meat or fowl, ending with cheese and dessert. Meals would dance with mussels swimming in egg-driven mustard mayonnaise in a large shell or grainy country pâté, to gooey cheese-topped French onion soup, cordon bleu, rack of New Zealand lamb and quail with grapes covered with light wine sauce. All entrées were served on plates heated on tableside carts.

With John in the kitchen, Smith ran the front of house, acting as maître d' and bartender, confidently suggesting $1.50 tulip glasses of Lillet splashed with cognac and a twist of orange peel.

"Dining at La Truffe is like the time you bought a whole bag of the best chocolate chip cookies money can buy and ate them all at one sitting—thinking it was delicious, but sinful," reported Julia Lawlor for the *Daily News* in 1977.

Even Georges Perrier was a regular, recommending that he enjoyed the shrimp curry as one of his favorite dishes while dining out on days off.

Ten years in, La Truffe imported a world-class chef, Jean-François Taquet, from the restaurant Girardet in Switzerland.

In 1995, La Truffe won the 1994 Dinner of the Year Award as appointed by the Philadelphia chapter of Confrerie de la Chaine des Rotisseurs, a multinational society dedicated to the proper preparation and consumption of fine food. Throughout the year, the society members would attend and judge gourmet dinners across the city, and at the year's end, the best dinner was chosen.

The year 1994 was an exceptionally good one for La Truffe. It also nabbed placement in *Condé Nast Traveler*'s Top 50 Restaurants of America issue, securing fifteenth place. The restaurant also was featured on the Food Network's *TV Diners* show in October of the same year.

Annually, La Truffe would host a Bastille Day party, which included, as Mermet relayed in July 1996 to the *Inquirer*, "a lot of singing and dancing—and the same people came every year."

After twenty-five years of service, Mermet and Smith closed La Truffe in the fall of 1996. Jeannine Mermet went on to teach cooking classes out of her Bala Cynwyd home in collaboration with one-time La Truffe chef, Thierry Vergnault. In 1998, Smith and Mermet also tried their hand at a Mediterranean restaurant, Sienna, on Delaware Avenue in Wilmington.

Through La Truffe's time, its kitchen acted as a breeding ground for up-and-coming chefs, many of whom went on to open their own restaurants, like George Honzik and Ted Polish with now-closed Bonjour at Fourth and Bainbridge Streets or Edward Seitel with his now-closed Chez Patou at Twentieth and Lombard Streets.

PART II

ONE BUILDING, A DOZEN ACCOLADES

9

Walk Down Memory Lane

I t's common for one building to be the home of many restaurants. Ambitious chefs and their restaurant concepts come and go, but there is one address—1312 Spruce Street—that could hold the trophy for housing some of the city's most iconic and acclaimed restaurants, many of which were French.

Prior to Marc Vetri introducing his namesake Italian restaurant to the charmed Washington Square West townhouse in 1998, there was a steady line of chefs that prospered well before him in the same four walls.

"It's clearly got a great vibe," Vetri told *Billy Penn* in 2015. "When I first walked in, I literally knew in my bones that it was the place. I can't explain it…it was calling me."

HOME SWEET HOME, 1860–1960S

Following the Consolidation Act of 1854, which extended the city's borders to the perimeters of Philadelphia County and significantly expanded the city's population, Philly entered into a metropolitan rivalry with New York City. In true Philly fashion, it didn't spark the city to flood the area with high-rises; instead, developers continued to build small. Enter a 3,500-square-foot, three-story row home near Broad Street and Philadelphia's City Hall that would, years later, become home to city-defining chefs.

For almost a century, the charming row home acted as a private residence until the early 1900s, when it was split into apartments and professional offices.

FIRST RESTAURANT, LA PANETIÈRE, IS INTRODUCED, 1967–1970

Peter von Starck, credited for sparking the fine-dining renaissance in Philadelphia, was the first chef to see the row home's potential for a restaurant. Developer Leonard Levin, cited for being instrumental in the redevelopment of Society Hill, swayed von Starck to move into the ground-level location.

Then twenty-six years old and from Bryn Mawr, Pennsylvania, von Starck debuted his own French restaurant with a fierce determination to introduce haute cuisine in the city and would cook without any compromises. It was named La Panetière, which means an "ornamental cupboard for bread and rolls" in French, and he made sure to have a French antique cupboard for show. He spent several years working and training toward this goal, including spending time in France as a saucier and poissonnier in the beautiful hotel-restaurant Baumanière les Baux de Provence, one of the country's few Michelin-starred restaurants.

To start his venture, he set about convincing a then twenty-one-year-old French chef, George Perrier, to relocate to Philly to run his kitchen—relocate from Lyons, France, to be precise. (Von Starck and Perrier had worked together at Baumanière.) He also lined up a maître d' from Netherlands Queen's Garden.

Immediately, La Panetière was hailed as Philadelphia's finest. It was one of the first fine-dining restaurants to open in the city since Prohibition. It was uncompromisingly French, with no English translations on the menu. It was Philadelphia's first restaurant to be taken seriously. It made Philadelphians feel pampered, surrounded by tasteful, almost aristocratic trappings.

In 1971, Elaine Tait reported in the *Philadelphia Inquirer* that a visitor, a graduate of both Paris and London Cordon Bleu schools, commented that "she had found La Panetière a superb restaurant, worthy of French and better than those she'd encounter in New York."

The signature Scope de St. Jacque au Safran, a saffron-laced scallop soup, received endless praise. The dish that many considered the absolute best was the Mousse de Crevettes aux Julienne, a shrimp mousse, which had air-light shrimp bound in a ring mold with cream. The Terrine de Canard, a pâté of duck, was equally popular, and in pure luxurious fashion, many flocked to the beluga Malossol caviar on the menu.

"The liver was thinly sliced, sautéed, then sauced with shallots, white wine, butter and parsley. I was a line cook then and brought the dish with me when I opened Frog," reminisced fellow restaurateur Steven Poses about his favorite signature dish at La Panetière.

Three years in, after a clash of temperaments, Perrier and von Starck parted ways. This was when von Starck moved his restaurant to a larger space on Locust Street and Perrier stayed behind on Spruce, opening a place of his own in La Panetière's former location, which became the original location of Le Bec-Fin. When Perrier left, von Starck stepped right back into the kitchen.

The restaurant closed in 1985 following the death of its prominent restaurateur. It was left to his surviving mother and brother, who had no interest in carrying on the restaurant without Peter.

"He was the first to make a successful French restaurant in Philadelphia when no one else thought you could bring French cuisine to this town. The city owes him a lot. He did what nobody else did, and he did first," Georges Perrier told the *Daily News* following the death of von Starck.

In La Panetière's sixteen-year run, it inspired more than 450 restaurants to enter Philadelphia's playing field, designed to up the ante on quality food first and foremost over price. Years later, La Panetière continued to be, as the *Washington Post* reported, the "yardstick by which Philadelphia measured dining elegance."

NATIONAL CRITIC ACCLAIM FLOODS IN, LE BEC-FIN, 1970–1983

Georges Perrier's darling French restaurant, Le Bec-Fin, was his chance to step out on his own from the kitchen he'd come to know so well since coming to the states.

In a dining room accented with crystal chandeliers and gold-trimmed mirrors, Perrier served the finest food the city had ever seen. Galette de crabe and quenelles de brochet danced on tabletops, and when the chef sashayed around the dining room for hellos, people "oohed" and "ahhed."

In 1974, Craig Claiborne of the *New York Times* printed that Le Bec-Fin was the best restaurant on the East Coast, and folks continued to flock to see what all the fuss was about.

At the time, Perrier's $16 fixed-price menu was a scandal. When he raised it to $25, "all the Quakers in the Union League were having heart attacks," said Fritz Blank.

Rightfully so, Perrier took credit for attracting the highest caliber of talent to his kitchen. Among them, many have since gone on to open successful restaurants of their own. From Jean-Pierre Tardy, Chip Roman and *Top Chef* winner Nicholas Elmi to Jack McDavid and Shola Olunloyo, among others.

Like von Starck, Perrier itched to expand, and thus he moved to larger digs at 1523 Walnut Street in 1983, where he continued his claim-to-fame restaurant well into the 2000s. He was also receiving invitations to relocate to major cities like Manhattan and Los Angeles but was able to purchase his new Locust Street home—a space that quickly became known as the "most elegant."

THE FOLLOWING ACT TO LE BEC-FIN, TWO QUAILS, 1983–1988

French native Joel Assouline made a name for himself in the '80s with his Philadelphia caviar importing operation, Assouline & Ting. With Le Bec-Fin exiting its original location, and as one of his best customers, he thought it would be worthwhile to capitalize on the reputation and success of the then vacant dining room. And so he did and called it Two Quails.

Assouline brought in two chefs to run the kitchen its first few months; the pair happened to be a couple and had studied in France for nine months before continuing to carry on the torch of the space christened as a French restaurant. Chefs Lori Frank and Jon Weinrott partnered in the kitchen of the thirty-five-seat Two Quails in all its pastel elegance, serving a much more Americanized menu aside haute French-style dishes. For appetizers, they featured the likes of silver dollar–sized ravioli stuffed with domestic foie gras, littleneck clams and mussels in a saffron-laced cream sauce; the most expensive main course was a sirloin steak with forty cloves of garlic.

Eventually, the two chefs ended up parting ways with the proprietor due to ever-popular philosophical differences. They went on to work at Fairmount Firehouse, while Assouline trucked on for five more years.

"If you are going to try and fill Le Bec Fin's shoes, it helps to have someone with a Cinderella touch there," wrote Stan Hochman for the *Daily News* in November 1983.

Two Quails was a modest success, though it never garnered the rave reviews of its two predecessors. A review by the *Inquirer*'s Gerald Etter described the atmosphere there as "tense calm," and though he enjoyed the food, he noted that "there seemed to be a strained aura" about the place.

After five years, Assouline was ready to free himself from full-service dining and return to retail, searching for someone to take over the charming space. He found ready takers in chefs Bruce Lim and Francesco Martorella.

THE FRENCH BRIGADE REMAINS WITH CIBOULETTE, 1988–1992

When Joel Assouline was looking for a chef to take over what was the home of his Two Quails, he approached Bruce Lim, who at the time was one of Philadelphia's top chefs, running the kitchen at the Fountain at the Four Seasons Hotel. Lim, born in Singapore and trained in France, was in fact ready to open his own restaurant, so he left Four Seasons Hotel and brought along his sous chef Francesco Martorella to join him.

Lim named his restaurant Ciboulette (French for "chives") and specialized in classic French cuisine. Lim and Martorella minimized the décor of the petite forty-seat bistro, making it more austere and melding creamy walls, touches of lace and small, bright flower bouquets on each table.

They featured three different degustations: six courses for $60, four for $45 and "a kind of quick pre-theater meal" for $30. The menu items themselves didn't have prices (only the cost per tasting), which made it chic in its day. Quickly, the all-star chef duo garnered rave reviews in their first year. Sam Gugino of the *Philadelphia Daily News* reported that "food takes center stage here, and it gives a bravura performance" in his glowing December 1988 review; it would be his last, as he was leaving the city for a new job opportunity.

Continuing the fanfare, in 1989, *Esquire* named Ciboulette one of the country's best new restaurants. In 1990, both Lim and Martorella were named as two of America's best new chefs in *Food & Wine*—a list that included only ten chefs nationwide. The same year, Jim Quinn for the *Inquirer* reported, "There's nothing like the food you get in a restaurant where everything is prepared by two great chefs trying to do everything exactly right. And succeeding."

Guests delighted over Provence-inspired fare like foie gras slices and sweet potato puree; eggplant terrine layered with earthy goat cheese, roasted sweet red peppers and dill-flecked tomato butter; sweetbreads with asparagus, sweet peas and sherry vinegar; seafood bouillabaisse; and loin of veal with a skein of herb-sauced capellini and porcini mushrooms. Lim eschewed cream in favor of natural juices and fresh herbs and didn't have a freezer on site to help reinforce their mission for freshness.

"The three-tiered dessert cart was always a hit, layered with slices of dainty plum tart, fresh ripe berries and cream, and Austrian opera cake with slivers of gold leaf atop," retold *Billy Penn* decades later.

At the time of Ciboulette, it was common for reporters to digress that what distinguished the restaurant was "all of its entrees were served in appetizer portions," "dessert lovers will applaud the restaurant's small portions because they leave room for some fairly spectacular desserts" and "the menu choices were small, but artfully conceived and executed." It was encouraged that through a dinner, one would order multiple dishes—a practice now common but then new to the late '80s patron.

As *Billy Penn* relayed:

> *Lim, who once was the personal chef to the Beatles' George Harrison, liked the concept* [of small plates] *because light eaters could eat as little as they wished while those with bigger appetites could sample different things instead of filling up on one single entrée. Lim likened it to what was popular at dim sum restaurants in Philadelphia's Chinatown. Then, Lim confessed that he believed this way of dining was going to be the future. (He was right.)*

As with those before him, it came time to move his restaurant to a larger space, to the Bellevue, on the second floor in a 110-seat space. Lim would continue to run Ciboulette there all the way through 2001, while Martorella went on to work at the prestigious Ritz-Carlton and become the opening chef at Brasserie Perrier.

FRANCO-CHINESE FUSION INTRODUCED, CHANTERELLES, 1992–1998

In 1986, Philippe Chin, a native Parisian born to a French mother and Chinese father, landed in Philadelphia. (At eighteen, he entered L'École Hôtelière de Paris, a French restaurant school ranked one of the best. And at twenty-four, he started to work in West Chester, Pennsylvania, at La Cocotte.) After stints at the then Founders at the Bellevue and 210 at the Rittenhouse Hotel, he was ready to strike out on his own. Enter: Chanterelles on Spruce Street.

True to his roots, at the ripe age of thirty-two, Chin presented a Franco-Chinese fusion menu. At the time, Susanna Foo had started to introduce Philadelphians to her signature Asian dishes built with French ingredients, but it was Chin's intention to do the reverse. His dishes were elegant and romantic, serving fresh contemporized French dishes, including seared rare foie gras served with fresh gooseberry chutney and a twenty-five-year-old balsamic glaze; ginger-spiced blini and cream soup with shiitakes and venison with au poivre sauce; or skate with lemon butter and capers. His desserts were always new inventions, such as a bitter chocolate sorbet with exotic fruit relish and Asian-flavored syrup.

Chin's food brought a steady stream of accolades, including mentions in *Esquire, Gourmet* and *Bon Appétit* magazines and appearances on Food Network.

In 1996, *Philly Mag* named Chin one of the city's "hippest" people, suggesting the chef possessed a cool-guy swagger, driving a Harley and wearing cowboy boots around his restaurant. In 1997, he was admitted to the Maîtres Cuisiniers de France, making him the youngest French master chef at that time. The next year, the National Restaurant Association named him restaurateur of the year. By 1998, he was ready for a larger platform. He signed onto a project called Philippe on Locust and then set about finding someone to take over his 1312 Spruce lease. By 2002, he was off to the South eager for a warm place where he could do his thing. That "thing" became the restaurant Bambu, where he served arctic char with furikake sticky rice and wasabi mashed potatoes.

In 2012, he resurfaced on the East Coast in Somers Point, New Jersey, with a three-hundred-seat namesake restaurant and deck bar.

VETRI FINDS HIS FAVORITE HOME, 1998–TODAY

Like his predecessors, it was time for Abington, Pennsylvania native Marc Vetri to open his first solo venture. The Spruce Street restaurant, with its endless historical acclaim, felt like the right place to do so. At the age of thirty-one, opening his own restaurant was everything to him, and it was totally putting himself on the line. Up until then, he had been a local and national star, splashed on the pages of *Bon Appétit* magazine and acclaimed by the James Beard Foundation.

Vetri plowed all of his savings into the thirty-eight-seat restaurant. He didn't have any backers, and for the first two months back in Philadelphia from New York, where he was working as executive chef of Bella Blu, he slept on the floor of his new restaurant.

This time, however, the Spruce Street restaurant wasn't going to be French inspired but rather rustic Italian, and his décor reflected just that: the rolling hills of Italy. He had a love for Italian cooking since Sundays in his boyhood when his grandmother would prepare Sicilian feasts in her South Philadelphia home.

Vetri continues to have an effect on Philadelphia. Through the years, critics have suggested, "Vetri is expensive, completely over the top, and possibly the best restaurant in Philadelphia [yet] 'long live the king' proclaim supporters of fine-dining patriarch Marc Vetri, whose eponymous Washington Square West flagship takes Italian to a new level, one so sublime the experience becomes more fantasy than restaurant."

PART III

THE AUTOMAT AND RISE

OF CAFETERIA DINING

10
Horn & Hardart's

Philadelphia, a city where the ambitious patented such things as cast-iron stoves, Mason jars and ice cream makers, is also home to the industrial innovation that is fast food.

On December 22, 1888, Joseph V. Horn and Frank Hardart opened their first coin-operated, chrome-lined cafeteria at 39 South Thirteenth Street. Some would argue this was the beginning of the fast-food era. The duo, eventually naming their business after themselves, Horn & Hardart's, purveyed ready-made lunches to workers of all classes. It was a cavernous, waiter-less establishment that would become known and famous for foods purchased by placing a coin in the slot and removing the food found behind a small glass window.

Eventually, they would grow into the world's largest chain, serving more than 800,000 a day in the Northeast with locations beyond Philadelphia, including New York—which was introduced in 1912.

They called their cafeteria-style dining an "automat." The word *automat* comes from the Greek *automatos*, meaning "self-acting," but their automats weren't entirely automatic, as the locations were heavily staffed. The second a customer removed a sandwich from the glass slot, a staff member behind the machine would quickly refill it. There was never a vacated chamber.

They had a strict fresh-food policy, too. No food would be left overnight in any of its restaurants—or its retail shops (whose motto was "Less Work

Historic postcard illustrating the Horn & Hardart's dining room lined with vending machines, 1906. *Courtesy of the Library Company of Philadelphia.*

for Mother"). After closing each day, Horn & Hardart's trucks carried surplus food to day-old shops. New York and Philadelphia each had three, located in low-income neighborhoods, which sold these items at reduced prices. Automats also enforced quality control. There was a leather-bound rule book every manager received listing the proper handling of nearly four hundred menu items. Within the pages, each meal item was outlined by where to position the buffet-style food on the plates and stated the number of times employees needed to wipe tabletops each day.

Every day, founders Horn and Hardart and other executives lunched together at the Sample Table (or the "ulcer table," as coined by some disgruntled employees). They did so to test the day's quality and uniformity. They would also sit and judge whether new ingredients from outside suppliers were superior or inferior to what they currently used.

There were no tables, only a counter and stools. The style of dining was new to Philadelphia, borrowed successfully from Germany. For those truly in a rush, there were stand-up counters too, with those hurried business folks becoming known as enjoying "perpendicular meals."

Patrons were discouraged from tipping. Nor did any cash register reveal the cost of a meal for all to see; the coin slots kept thrifty customers' dining expenditures discreetly hidden. Philadelphia's automats were haunts for

HOW AN AUTOMAT WORKS

FIRST DROP YOUR NICKELS IN THE SLOT

THEN TURN THE KNOB THE GLASS DOOR CLICKS OPEN

LIFT THE DOOR AND HELP YOURSELF

HORN & HARDART

Interior of One of the Fifty Automat-Cafeterias in Philadelphia and New York

Horn & Hardart's "How an automat works" postcard, 1950. *Courtesy of the Library Company of Philadelphia.*

actors, hotel guests and merchants along Jewelers Row, as well as blue-collar workers and everyday folks. The restaurants didn't hustle guests out who lingered over their meal—or even those who didn't buy food.

Automats were something special to children. They would obtain nickels from cashiers located in glass booths who wore rubber tips on their fingers and were called "nickel throwers." With a handful of change, they could choose a meal from foods they liked.

In an August 2001 article in *Smithsonian Magazine*, Carolyn Hughes Crowley described the appeal of the automat as a place where "customers scooped up their nickels, slipped them into in the coin slots and turned the chrome-plated knobs with their porcelain centers. In a few seconds the compartment next to the slot revolved into place to present the desired cold food to the customer through a small glass door that opened and closed."

A menu from 1940 from the New York Public Library indicated that one could get a choice of juice, fruit cup or cereal, as well as eggs prepared any style or griddle cakes or eggs with bacon and home fried potatoes and toast for twenty-five cents. A complete breakfast special could be purchased for fifteen cents.

Actor Gregory Peck claimed that Horn & Hardart's had the best scrambled eggs in the world, and his other favorites included creamed spinach, Salisbury steak, Harvard beets and apple brown betty. Automat food was "good and wholesome and had an all-American, home-economist feeling about it," said Mimi Sheraton, a former dining critic for the *New York Times*.

Others raved over their macaroni and cheese, baked beans and navy beans as staple offerings.

Horn & Hardart's coffee was a popular item. In their '50s heyday, automats sold more than ninety million cups of fresh-brewed coffee each year poured out of silver, wall-mounted dolphin heads. From 1912 to 1950, a cup cost a nickel. Horn & Hardart's introduced the first fresh drip-brewed coffee to Philadelphia and New York. Before then, coffee on the East Coast had been a harsh drink made by boiling it interminably with eggshells to clarify it. After brewing each batch of their coffee, Horn & Hardart's employees filled out a timecard. After twenty minutes, they discarded whatever coffee remained and prepared more.

Irving Berlin, the composer of "God Bless America," wrote a famous song about this delicious brew, "Let's Have Another Cup of Coffee," which became Horn & Hardart's theme song.

In December 17, 2012, writer Glenn Collins published the article "The Automat May Be Long Gone, but Its Recipes Are in Demand," within it a complete recipe for the preparation of Horn & Hardart's baked beans.

In 2012, Laura Shapiro and Rebecca Federman curated the *Lunch Hour NYC* exhibition at the New York Public Library on Fifth Avenue. During that time, more than 500,000 free automat recipes have been snapped up by visitors. "Those recipes evoke people's memories more than anything else in the show," said Federman. The automat recipes were a closely guarded secret until the '60s. Federman and Shapiro discovered them in their research and offered them in the show.

Horn & Hardart's started to decline in the late '60s. (However, this didn't stop them, as by the mid-'60s, they had opened fifty-five retail outlets and forty-four restaurants in the Philadelphia region, including New Jersey and Delaware.) The early concept of Horn & Hardart's disappeared in the early '90s, although there were several private efforts to resurrect. Horn & Hardart's notable South Broad Street location closed in May 1983 after sixty years in business. In its heyday, it grossed more than $1 million a year, but once the '80s hit, it was said that "running a cafeteria at the corner of Broad and Walnut streets wasn't the highest use of the space."

Automats fell victim to changing tastes. When cafeteria-style food became out of fashion and others no longer ate a full meal at lunch,

Inside the Horn & Hardart's at Thirty-Fourth and Walnut Streets. *Courtesy of Penn Archives.*

automats suffered. As Americans moved into the suburbs and didn't travel into the city as frequently, automats' night business suffered too. Expense account dining rooms fueling the clientele of the '70s restaurant renaissance replaced the popularity of businessmen dining at cafeteria-style restaurants. As history unfolded, in the '70s, Horn & Hardart's dying restaurants were replaced with Burger King franchises. Those who loved the charm of automats' fancy fixtures and diverse menu were a diamond in the rough. Upscale power lunchers' elevated palates didn't call automats home.

The last Horn & Hardart's automats closed in 1991, in both Philadelphia and New York. Passionate to breathe fresh life into the Horn & Hardart's brand, the Mazzone family invested in them after brick-and-mortar closures, selling a range of the favorite recipes in supermarkets. Eventually, in 2009, the family acquired all rights to the Horn & Hardart's name and recipes and decided to focus solely on the coffee, duplicating the original H&H coffee blend that coffee drinkers have enjoyed for over a century.

Horn & Hardart's fanatics can find a piece of Philadelphia's history in the Smithsonian's National Museum of American History, where a thirty-five-foot piece of Philadelphia's 1902 Horn & Hardart's is in residence, beautifully ornate with its mirrors, marble and marquetry.

Lorraine B. Diehl and Marianne Hardart published a 2002 book titled *The Automat*, which goes deep into the restaurants' history and the effect the automat had on the East Coast dining culture.

Horn & Hardart's Recipe: Baked Macaroni and Cheese
From the New York Public Library
Serves 4

¼ pound elbow macaroni
1 ½ tablespoons butter
1 ½ tablespoons flour
½ teaspoon salt
Dash white pepper, red pepper
1 ½ cups milk
2 tablespoons light cream
1 cup Cheddar cheese, shredded
½ teaspoon sugar
½ cup canned diced tomatoes

Cook macaroni according to directions on the package. Preheat oven to 400 degrees. Melt butter in the top of a double boiler. Blend flour, salt and white and red pepper in gradually. When smooth, add milk and cream, stirring constantly. Cook for a few minutes until it thickens.

Add cheese and continue to heat until it melts and the sauce looks smooth. Remove from heat. Add cooked macaroni to the sauce. Add sugar to the tomatoes and add to the sauce. Pour mixture into a buttered baking dish and bake until the surface browns.

11

The Colonnade

Locations: 1616 Walnut Street; 125 South Juniper Street; 28 South Sixth Street within the Rohn & Haas Building

The Colonnade Co. started in Cleveland in 1911. Over time, the Colonnade Co. expanded its footprint to a number of cities, including Pittsburgh, Newark, Cincinnati, Houston and Detroit. Known as a cafeteria pioneer, the Colonnade was the first to develop and use the hollow square principle of serving food while eliminating the usual fixed line. It also maintained an extensive food research laboratory that tested and selected all new foods to be featured throughout the following year.

The Colonnade Cafeteria was a destination and Philadelphia institution for wholesome, moderately priced fare, known for $2.95 lunches and $4.00 Wednesday night dinners. It would serve lunch to 1,000 people each weekday, from 11:00 a.m. to 2:00 p.m. At the height of its popularity, the Juniper location served 3,200 patrons at lunchtime every single day. It remained a wholesome constant, continuing to serve quality food at an affordable price and not caving to serve newer fashions in food or fit contemporary lifestyles.

A typical day's menu offered five to six entrées, eleven vegetables and from-scratch desserts. It was constantly changing. For four dollars, you could get a full-course dinner of an entrée, two vegetables, dessert, a beverage and a roll and butter.

A range of options included calf's liver, roast prime rib, stuffed Cornish game hen, veal loaf, eggplant, collard greens with bacon, chicken noodle or lentil soup, chef's salad and lemon meringue pie or apple pie. Occasionally, there was a surprise to the diner, like a twenty-five-cent bowl of alfalfa sprouts.

"There was no place in town where you could get this kind of food," relayed Joseph Callahan, Colonnade's manager in 1984. "It was first-rate cafeteria food prepared under the supervision of a trained dietitian."

At the height of the self-service cafeterias, they were exclusive to big cities, scarce in the suburbs, where fast food was king. Over time, its locations grew in Philadelphia, with destinations at Sixteenth and Walnut, Juniper and Sixth and Market Streets.

Rita Cardillo was an employee of the Colonnade location at Sixth and Market for more than twenty-one years. Her two-decade stint started in 1963 and included running the service counter and showing customers to their seats.

"The same people came here for years," Cardillo recalled to the *Inquirer* in 1984. "They would come and sit here for hours. We had a good class of clientele. The customer got comfort and value, and they didn't have to tip."

A benefit of the Colonnade locations was the fact that you didn't have to wait for a server. You'd look at the food and decide what you wanted, it would be given to you and you'd take it to your seat.

Downtown Colonnade locations were frequented by high-profile Philadelphians, including judges and anchors of local broadcast stations. When KYW resided downtown at Fifth and Market, the Colonnade was right across the street to welcome celebrity guests who would come by before or after their appearances at the station.

In January 1985, the Colonnade Cafeteria at 1616 Walnut Street closed after fifty-three years of service due to an increase in rent. (This location was acquired by Temple University.)

In September 1985, the last remaining Colonnade Cafeteria closed. "With the growth of fast-food restaurants in the area, there just isn't a need for a larger, full-service restaurant," reported the *Inquirer* at the time of its closing.

During the Colonnade's heyday, it had more than eleven locations in Philadelphia and scattered across the Midwest and Texas.

PART IV

SEAFOOD-SLINGING SHOWSTOPPERS

12
Striped Bass

1500 Walnut Street

Before Stephen Starr oversaw a national empire of more than thirty-five restaurants, he helmed one of Walnut Street's swankier turn-of-the-century destinations. But it wasn't Stephen Starr who debuted the seafood palace. The Striped Bass's introduction came by way of its original former co-owners Neil Stein and Joe Wolf. From May 1994 to 2003, the duo's Striped Bass graced the expense account set with a seafood-centric menu, heavy on the truffles and champagne.

It was not an easy start. The restaurant took an eternity to open, which required a move from where it was originally planned to start at 2601 Pennsylvania Avenue to its location on Walnut Street. However, Walnut Street came with its share of headaches and cost a fortune (roughly $2.5 million) to transform former brokerage offices into the partners' elaborate seafood-laden dream.

Co-owner Wolf said, "People told us it would be suicide, an all-fish restaurant." But it didn't work out that way—and they kept going for it.

In 1994, Beth D'Addono reported for the *Courier Post* that Striped Bass could be thought of as a "culinary theater.…That's what patrons can expect from the chef's table feasts offered seven days a week." D'Addono wasn't the only one who buzzed about the elite restaurant. *Bon Appétit, Town & Country* and *Esquire* provided them with national glossy magazine press.

The buzz, among the restaurant's brilliance, pushed Philadelphians to all want an immediate piece of the action—even if it required a whole paycheck. Then it would require a diner six weeks to secure a reservation on a Saturday night. At the time, couples largely would only go out for a night of theater and dinner, but people began to shift to making dining out a sole event. Restaurants replaced the popularity of private clubs; restaurants became more theatrical, and people went out to eat to be seen.

Philadelphia Magazine owner Herb Lipson once said that he went to Striped Bass "to feel good in that room. It was elegant. It was a room filled with people who look good."

Le Bec-Fin's owner Georges Perrier was quoted as saying, "It was the best thing to have happened to Walnut Street." (Le Bec-Fin was a neighbor.) Striped Bass once published an ad that read, "Across the street is America's greatest chef (if we could only get him out of our restaurant)."

Patrons fought fiercely for the eight tables that were center stage, especially those that were directly in the center.

The dining room was built around a $300,000 exhibition kitchen that ran across the back wall, in full view for the entire restaurant to see the star of the show—the chef alongside seven sous chefs—in action, preparing as many as 350 dinners a night. The chef's table was said to offer the best seats in the house, set in the middle of all the action in the main dining area (unlike La Truffe nearby, which offered a chef's dinner in its private upstairs room).

"Having people so close to the chef in some ways disrupts the kitchen's routine, but that's the excitement of it all," shared co-owner Neil Stein six months into opening Striped Bass. "The chef's table [allowed] us to attract some of the best talent in the business—it created an incredible atmosphere for them to work—they're not locked up in some back room somewhere, they're onstage."

And what a space it was. Besides the open kitchen, the restaurant was visually stunning, with marble columns, draped fabrics and a grandiose metal sculpture of a striped bass named Max. The menu itself was printed daily, both fresh for lunch and dinner. There was a mahogany bar that sat eighteen guests, tucked away in the restaurant's northeast corner, but it typically was flooded with forty or more imbibers, some of whom were regulars who spent near $5,000 a month.

"Striped Bass [lifted] you out of your own space. It was larger than life, like a movie set," said Meryl Levitz, when she was the vice president of tourism development for the Philadelphia Convention & Visitors Bureau. "It [was] reminiscent of a big-city restaurant in New York, Chicago or L.A. It's instant that you're in a different place."

"People came to Striped Bass and they didn't feel like they were in Philadelphia anymore," shared Striped Bass's former assistant manager Randi Sirkin.

As Karen Heller elaborated in a 1994 issue of the *Philadelphia Inquirer*, "Striped Bass' success disproves several generalizations often lobbed at Philadelphians: that they're cheap, impatient, indifferent to their surroundings, and would never take to a place that has the temerity to serve a $20 salad and not a single shred of beef."

Dining at Striped Bass during its premier year, you could expect lunch at the chef's table to range from $25 to $35 and dinner $50 to $85—not including wine. The chef's table was exquisite, shiny mahogany set with Villeroy & Boch china, as well as silver and crystal.

The napkins were brand-new every day. The restaurant paid a lot for them, but it guaranteed that there were no stains. "You see stains, it's bad for business," quipped Stein during his heyday. Striped Bass spent $3,000 a week on flowers. The chef rejected any fish that was proved to be inferior. Wolf repainted the wall twice a week to guarantee there were never any nicks showing.

An unforgettable meal at Striped Bass, which was awarded one of the highest four-bell reviews by the *Philadelphia Inquirer*'s Craig LaBan, would have most likely gone like this: The meal debuts with an assortment of cheese and fruit, followed by butlered hors d'oeuvres and an appetizer course. Steamed shrimp dumplings and tuna ceviche were raved meal-starters, with fresh fish flown in from the Gulf of Mexico. Entrées were black channel bass prepared in a red wine sauce with wild mushrooms, leeks and potatoes; soft shell crabs served with pesto linguine and red peppers; grouper baked with macadamia nut crush and pineapple salsa; and ginger-fried squid flavored with coriander and tomato.

Then in early 2003, Stephen Starr made a bid to buy Striped Bass, which was operating in bankruptcy. Starr submitted a bid of $1.3 million to purchase the restaurant, going on the record that he would not alter the restaurant's name or motif. (In June 2003, Neil Stein lost control of the restaurant under terms of a bankruptcy agreement.) Starr's Striped Bass rose quickly to the head of the class, continuing the elegance of sophisticated seafood dishes that popped with great ingredients, clever ideas and exceptionally modern executions.

Starr brought notable chef Alfred Portale in to head the kitchen, a chef known for popularizing "tall food," an idea of layering flavors and giving food motion on a plate. He also possessed wit, which was illustrated through his execution of his playful brainchild, the "Philadelphia cheese stake." His reinvention of a haute cheesesteak was executed through braised short ribs sandwiched with mushrooms and caramelized pearl onions inside folds of skate that was encrusted with bread crumbs. It was plated with a swirl of Parmesan and a touch of homemade hot sauce.

Overall, the entrées offered by the new Striped Bass were slightly less expensive, topping out at around the mid-thirties per dish. They were also noticeably more generous with their serving sizes.

Craig LaBan confessed that while in many cases it was an improvement over its predecessor, it did face the challenge of shedding its early starch to rediscover the sultry energy of the city's most glamorous dining room.

In June 2008, Starr announced plans that Striped Bass would close and become the more expensive, '40s supper club–style steakhouse Butcher & Singer, which continues to operate today. (The name Butcher & Singer actually harkened the former brokerage offices that filled the space prior to the Striped Bass.)

13

The Original Snockey's Oyster & Crab House

1020 South Second Street

On May 3, 1912, twenty-year-old Polish immigrant Frank Snock, an oyster shucker, noticed a restaurant that had closed down on South Street and went to his boss with the suggestion that he should take it over and expand. His boss, not interested in a second location, suggested Snock should open it *himself*. And so he did. A mercantile license then cost him $1.75.

The restaurant opened during the presidency of William Howard Taft, and the biggest thing on the planet happening at the time was the *Titanic* setting sail. Opening day was memorable, as Frank's wife, Rose, was pregnant; she worked for a bit at the restaurant until she went upstairs to go into labor. Two days later, she was back in the kitchen, and there she remained, working every day until she was seventy-nine years old, in 1991.

Philadelphians were big consumers of oyster houses, with locals commonly eating a dozen a week at one of the many oyster-slinging restaurants speckled throughout the city. Years later, Frank's grandson Skip would relay to the *Philadelphia Inquirer* that it was bold of his grandfather to open an oyster house at that time, as "there were probably as many oyster houses in Philadelphia as delicatessens in New York." While there may have been many oyster houses, Frank Snock's place was special—it stood the test of time for 103 years, until it closed in 2015.

As early as the 1870s, raw oysters were a *thing* in Philadelphia, with some 2,419 Philadelphia hotels, oyster houses, restaurants and saloons serving

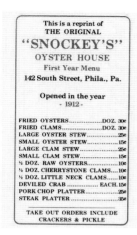

This is a reprint of
THE ORIGINAL
"SNOCKEY'S"
OYSTER HOUSE
First Year Menu
142 South Street, Phila., Pa.

Opened in the year
- 1912 -

FRIED OYSTERS	DOZ. 30¢
FRIED CLAMS	DOZ. 30¢
LARGE OYSTER STEW	25¢
SMALL OYSTER STEW	15¢
LARGE CLAM STEW	25¢
SMALL CLAM STEW	15¢
½ DOZ. RAW OYSTERS	10¢
½ DOZ. CHERRYSTONE CLAMS	10¢
½ DOZ. LITTLE NECK CLAMS	10¢
DEVILED CRAB	EACH. 15¢
PORK CHOP PLATTER	25¢
STEAK PLATTER	35¢

TAKE OUT ORDERS INCLUDE
CRACKERS & PICKLE

A reprint of the first-year menu of Original Snockey's Oyster & Crab House, which opened in 1912. *Courtesy of Snockey's Oyster House.*

them daily. That did not count the roving peddlers and curbside stands, either. But by the late 1950s, 95 percent of the Delaware Bay's oysters had been wiped out by disease, and with the drop-off of local oysters, oyster houses began to fold. But not the Snock family's.

However, the restaurant did experience its fair share of moves. After their first six years on South Street, in 1918, the seafood slingers relocated to Second and Fitzwater and then near Eighth and South from 1931 until 1975. They again were forced to move because the Crosstown Expressway was going to be built right through their restaurant. For seven years, they hired lawyers to fight the eminent domain claim, but they were eventually forced out in 1975. (For the history buffs, the expressway ended up never being built.) Their final move to the old Queen Village Inn location, at South Second Street, was where they stayed for the last forty years of service.

The last location ended up being where they belonged, run by the family for three generations. "This neighborhood is where Frank and Rose grew up," Skip shared with the *Philadelphia Inquirer* in 2014. "They knew this neighborhood. Everyone in this area was Polish. My grandmother came into this country two blocks away from here, at the foot of Washington Avenue. It's where all the immigrants came ashore."

A great meal at Snockey's started with a half-dozen or a dozen oysters. Over time, the oyster menu expanded to thirteen different varieties. Co-owner Skip Snock suggested that in their century of operating the restaurant, they most likely sold ten million oysters, calculating roughly three thousand oysters sold per week and three hundred sold a day.

Beyond oysters, shellfish was what Snockey's did best: lobster, scallops, shrimp, crab, oysters, clams and mussels. They were all prepared fresh and either fried, sautéed or broiled. You wouldn't find anything fancy—no mahi mahi or Ahi tuna—and they were old school, with endless orders of flounder, bluefish, salmon and tilapia. In an *Inquirer* ad from 1948, they billed the restaurant as having "jumbo crabs, all year 'round, lobsters, steamed clams, and fine beer." You may have found tilapia Francaise on the menu, but that was as fancy as it got.

Historic postcard of the Original Snockey's Oyster & Crab House, acclaimed for its famous hard-shell crabs. *Courtesy of Penn Archives Collection.*

The Snocks believed their strict attention to tradition helped their restaurant prosper through the years. No oyster mignonette, reductions or any funny business made a mark in this kitchen. They didn't follow trends; there was complete lack of pretense.

The old school seafood house, with even its most loving reviews singling out its "distinct smell" or "gruff service," was known for its inexpensive raw bar offerings, all-you-can-eat crab leg nights and "Clammy Hours," the best oyster deals in town—you could have a half-dozen raw mollusks for 90¢ apiece. (For a *long* time before that, they were 83¢ apiece. When the restaurant opened in 1912, a half-dozen oysters would be a total of 10¢.)

Another happy hour bargain was the Clammy Mary, a Bloody Mary in a pint glass that was loaded to the brim and topped with a skewer of three just-shucked littlenecks.

The location was right near Washington Avenue and the Mummer's Museum. Locals loved to chase down a dozen oysters with a Yuengling porter or two and watch all the neighbors pass through and trade barbs with the staff.

Through its century of operating, the oyster house passed down from generation to generation, with third-generation owners brothers Ken and Skip Snock being the final pair to run the show. (They had started at the

The Original Snockey's Oyster & Crab House was owned by generations of Snocks, with brothers Skip (*left*) and Ken Snock (*right*), serving customers until the restaurant's final days in 2015. *Courtesy of* Philadelphia Inquirer.

restaurant washing dishes and shucking oysters as soon as they could reach the sink.) They both lived in Cape May County and would commute to Philly nearly every day to make sure their Queen Village institution continued to run smoothly.

Eventually, in their sixties, the Snock brothers decided to step away from the business, preparing it for sale as early as late 2014 due to skyrocketing real estate values. They closed in 2015 after 104 years.

The Original Snockey's Oyster & Crab House Recipe: Mrs. Snockey's Original Oyster Stew

This stew would arrive tableside seconds after the oysters' edges began to curl—the "most critical moment to perfect."

Makes 1 serving

8 medium stewing oysters, shucked
4 ounces oyster liquor
4 ounces clam juice
6 ounces heavy cream
1 teaspoon melted butter
Salt, pepper and celery salt to taste
Optional for serving: oyster crackers or pepper hash

In a medium saucepan over medium-high heat, combine the oysters, oyster liquor and clam juice and cook, stirring frequently, just until the oysters begin to curl at the edges. Do not allow it to boil. Transfer to a large serving bowl and cover to keep warm.

In a small saucepan over medium heat, combine the heavy cream and butter and cook until steaming but not boiling. Slowly stir the cream mixture into the oyster mixture and season with salt, pepper and celery salt. Serve immediately with OTC (Original Trenton Crackers).

14

Old Original Bookbinder's

125 Walnut Street

Chef Jose Garces might have had historical preservation in mind when he took over the iconic Bookbinder's building between Front and Second on Walnut Street in 2015. But no modern-day incarnation could hold a torch to the Old Original Bookbinder's.

The stately restaurant and bar pleased Philadelphians for generations—for 110 years, to be exact.

It's hard to find a Philadelphia native over the age of forty who doesn't have a cherished Bookbinder's memory. It held the trophy for the world's largest indoor lobster tank and pushed a retro menu full of deviled crabs, herring in sour cream and oysters Rockefeller.

The restaurant's history can be traced to an oyster saloon that opened in 1893 on Fifth Street, near South Street, by a Dutch-Jewish immigrant Samuel Bookbinder. In 1898, Bookbinder moved his restaurant to Second and Walnut Streets to be closer to the docks on the Delaware River. This location thrived due to its proximity to the ingredients, including the river that teemed with shad, terrapin and schooners docked at port with cargoes of spices. The Chesapeake Bay also offered its bounty of oysters, crabs and clams, while fresh produce arrived daily from the fields surrounding Philadelphia.

As its history told, each noontime, Samuel's wife, Sarah, would ring the restaurant's bell, announcing the meal of the day. (Sarah's bell, although silent, remained standing inside the entranceway of Bookbinder's for years as a tribute to the uninterrupted tradition of great dining.) Dockworkers would float to the restaurant, rubbing elbows with sea captains, merchants, stockbrokers and farmers. The early-on intermingling of different classes painted the future of what Bookbinder's would become, a destination for all walks of life, no matter what job you held.

Bookbinder's location was surrounded by Old City Philadelphia charm: cobblestone streets and colonial brick houses—much of which remains today. The bustling restaurant was passed to the Bookbinder children and stayed in the family until the Depression era, when it was bequeathed to the Jewish Federated Charities.

Eventually, in 1941, it was acquired by John Taxin, who was a local produce business owner with an affinity for the restaurant and had enjoyed many midday meals there. (According to city records, the purchase was made with partners Hyman B. Sichel and Jimmy Retana, who were soon bought out a few years later.)

In 1949, Taxin added "Old Original" to the restaurant's name to differentiate it from the Bookbinder's Seafood House that was opened by two of Samuel Bookbinder's grandsons in 1935 on Fifteenth Street near Locust in a former police precinct building dating to 1890. (Rumor has it that following a bitter family dispute over one of the Bookbinders' sons marrying a non-Jewish woman who waitressed at the restaurant, the second competing Bookbinder's opened on Fifteenth Street.)

Taxin took pride in remodeling the restaurant and growing eatery both for size and its reputation. Over his run, the bar and restaurant included three bars, seven dining rooms and seating for eight hundred, sprawling into a fifty-four thousand-square-foot structure that eventually took up most of Walnut Street between Front and Second.

Most memorable was the restaurant's décor, decorated with bas-reliefs of dead U.S. presidents on its stained-glass façade and the Gettysburg Address written in bronze near the front door. The lobby held the site's crown jewel: what was said to be the "world's largest indoor lobster tank," able to accommodate 350 lobsters at a time. There were ship models and taxidermy game fish speckled throughout the walls. The most notable dining room, President's Room, was preserved to its original condition, wood-paneled and lined with big round tables ringed by captain's chairs, including photographs of the first forty-two presidents on its walls.

"You will immediately be struck by the huge, freestanding aquarium and its colorful tropical residents," wrote Jim Anderson in his book *Philly's Best Bars, 1992*, noting this made the trip worth it alone. "There [were] also large

Inside Old Original Bookbinder's stately dining room. *Courtesy of Penn Archives.*

collections of toy fire engines and antique pistols and rifles in display, as well as hundreds of photos of the current owners with their famous clientele."

Neil Stein, a known Philadelphia restaurateur, once said, "It was the first restaurant here to have a 'big pound,' a huge wooden tank. The aroma was just fantastic. John Taxin and his cronies sat at the same round table in the bar every day at lunch and smoked cigars. And if you weren't there, your seat was empty."

As legend has it, John and Jean Taxin tried to touch every table in the dining room, whether the diners were one-off visitors or regulars.

Over time, Bookbinder's became endearingly known as Bookie's, a place that particularly captivated celebrities, tourists and the clubby crowd of Philadelphians who went there for long, martini-splashed lunches, birthdays and anniversaries. It was during its heyday, from the '50s to the '70s, that red-jacketed waiters scurried through paneled rooms to tend to the rich and famous in town, from Diamond Jim Brady, Howard Cosell, Muhammad Ali and David Bowie to Gregory Peck, Julius Erving and John Wayne.

Gus De Pasquale, a waiter for fifty-two years, peeled behind the curtain of what it was like working at Bookbinder's:

I was fourteen when I started as a busboy. When we first started, it was all girls working as waitresses, because of the war. In the late '40s, Jack Klugman waited tables with me—Quincy! Abbott and Costello came in around that time, too. "Which was the fat one? Costello?" He used to chase Frances, one of the waitresses, around the dining room. She was a little heavyset, and he liked to pinch her. And they'd insult the people at the next table. Elizabeth Taylor came in many times when she was married to Eddie Fisher. She sat at Table 33 in the bar, and she'd eat lobster. She came in one time in a dress cut down to there, and Eddie Fisher would go like this to try to cover her up [makes motion of pulling a dress neckline up and together]. *Then she'd put it back.*

When you dined at Bookbinder's, there was always a chance that you would be served at a table once occupied by Babe Ruth, Tennessee Williams, Teddy Roosevelt or Al Jolson. Frank Sinatra routinely stopped by the restaurant whenever visiting Philadelphia, eventually earning himself a regular booth (no. 25) with his photo on it.

John Taxin once said, "I always liked it when people came back and said hi to the cooks and the dishwashers. Julius Erving did that, Muhammad Ali did that, and Frank Sinatra."

Politicians loved Bookie's, too. One day in 1972, the presidential helicopter landed in a dirt-topped parking lot across Walnut Street. To the amazement of patrons, President Richard Nixon had flown up from

Old Original Bookbinder's menu from 1957, one that celebrated its ninety years at the same address. *Courtesy of Penn Archives.*

Washington for a lunch date with the Philadelphia mayor at the time, Frank Rizzo. During John F. Kennedy's presidency, when he was in town for the Army-Navy game, he went to Bookbinder's and had the bouillabaisse. He loved it so much that he asked Taxin for the recipe. Taxin replied, "I'm sorry, Mr. President, but we can't give out the recipe. But I'll fly the soup down to the White House whenever you want."

Elliott Curson, a Philadelphia advertising executive, reminisced about his experiences dining with clients at Bookie's:

> *There were only a couple of places to eat back then—the Hunt Room in the Bellevue and the Vesper Club. Bookbinder's was two restaurants, really, one for Philadelphians and one for everyone else. If you walked into the restaurant and saw there were empty seats in the dining room but the bar was filled, you'd say, "Well, there's nowhere to sit." And you'd leave. It's like the Palm, where you have to sit on the left. The Taxins were part of the fun, having Albert and his father come to the table and kid around with you. They had a coffeepot out front for the drivers waiting outside. I'd always get the bluefish, and they had great salads and martinis. It was expensive, but it was good.*

Up until his retirement in the '80s, Taxin ran Bookbinder's with his son, Albert Taxin. Albert Taxin died of a brain tumor in 1993, and his son, John E., took over running the restaurant with Albert's sister, Sandy. (John M. Taxin died in 1997 at age ninety.)

In 1989, Bookbinder's began to feel the heat of restaurant competition, as the new age of buzzy dining destinations began to sprout. Prior to that, Bookbinder's spotlight reigned supreme, barely flinched against any other restaurant opening.

"In the '80s, it was still considered venerable, but we got this speeded-up Restaurant Renaissance in the '90s," said Meryl Levitz, founding president of Visit Philadelphia, to *Philadelphia Magazine*. "And all of a sudden there were all these new restaurants, and hotel restaurants got so good—there was competition everywhere." In September 1999, the *Inquirer* published a devastating review by Craig LaBan of both competing Bookbinder's restaurants. Old Original came off worse, receiving criticism for its prices and boiled-till-rubber lobsters. Still, it continued to press on.

Old Original continued to prosper nicely on its tourist trade and historic building. It had a gift shop that was stocked with everything from shot glasses to Beanie Babies, and its wall of celebrity photos remained up-to-date.

On New Year's Day 2002, John E. Taxin closed Bookbinder's doors. Years later, in 2005, after a $4.5 million renovation that added condominiums, a downsized version reopened. A bankruptcy filing came less than sixteen months after that. Among the main creditors were Renaissance Properties, its landlord; Royal Bank; and the Philadelphia Industrial Development Corporation, a private nonprofit organization founded by the city and the Greater Philadelphia Chamber of Commerce to promote economic development, which was owed about $650,000 from its $800,000 loan.

In 2006, the restaurant filed for protection under Chapter 11 of the U.S. Bankruptcy Code. At a hearing on April 29, 2009, Judge Eric L. Frank agreed with most creditors and the U.S. trustee that converting the case to Chapter 7, liquidating its assets under court supervision, would not be productive because of the high administrative costs. Old Original Bookbinder's bankruptcy petition was dismissed on April 29, 2009. Creditors, owed about $1.8 million, had to find a way outside of bankruptcy court to seek reimbursement from owners John E. Taxin and his aunt Sandy Taxin. In April 2009, John Taxin handed over the keys to the Old City landmark, which closed as he tried to find someone to save it. Albert A. Ciardi III, Bookbinder's bankruptcy attorney, said in May 2009 that two interested parties had come forward in the previous month but no sale had taken place.

The historical, renowned location sat dormant until it was reopened on January 9, 2015, by chef Jose Garces and the Garces Group (his ninth restaurant at the time). They named it Olde Bar, transforming the space into a mix of a seafood saloon and private catering event venue. (For private parties, there are rooms like the Vessel Room and the Blackburn Room, and the Commander's Room is known to host lobster boils and clambakes.) The Bookbinder's name and most of its historical woodwork and décor remained the same yet reimagined, still decked out with distinguished décor like the dead presidents' portraits and the Gettysburg Address written in bronze. The menu was similar, paying homage to the original's classic dishes with modern twists, but also touted a large raw bar.

Garces did keep some old hands on deck, including John Taxin's grandson Erich Weiss, who was hired to oversee the elevated cocktail program.

The Taxin family legacy continues with their Old Original Bookbinder's restaurant in Richmond, Virginia, which is located at 2306 East Cary Street.

In the early '70s, the Old Original Bookbinder's created a foods division, selling restaurant favorites packaged as convenient take-home products, including seafood soups, condiments and sauces. Silver Spring Foods Inc.

acquired the Bookbinder's Foods Division in 1999, while Bookbinder Specialties acquired the rights to the soups, bisques and seasonings in 2009.

Oh, and about the competing Bookbinder's on Fifteenth Street: it became famous for its snapper soup, Maine lobster and cheesecake. In the back was a Wall of Fame on which hung photos of celebrity guests who posed for pictures with Bookbinder family members over the years. However, after nearly seventy years on Fifteenth Street, Bookbinder's Seafood House fell into disrepair and closed. Newspaper reports indicate that tax problems and family squabbles did in the restaurant, which closed in 2003. Applebee's moved in soon after and operated until June 2020.

Old Original Bookbinder's Recipe: Snapper Soup

1 pound turtle meat or lean stewing beef
¼ cup butter
⅓ cup diced celery
⅓ cup diced onion
⅓ cup carrots
1 quart beef stock
1 teaspoon paprika
⅓ cup flour
½ cup tomato puree
1 clove garlic, crushed
½ teaspoon allspice
½ teaspoon salt
¼ teaspoon pepper
¼ teaspoon mixed pickling spice
3 tablespoons cornstarch
½ cup water
1 teaspoon Worcestershire sauce
1 teaspoon chopped parsley
⅓ cup cream sherry

Place turtle or beef in stockpot with 1½ quarts of water. Bring to a boil. Skim during cooking. Simmer for 2 hours or until meat is tender. Strain meat from stock. Dice meat into ¼-inch pieces. Set both aside.

Cook vegetables in butter until onions are translucent. Add beef stock.

In a small bowl, mix ¼ cup water into paprika and flour until smooth. Add tomato puree and spices. Stir into beef stock until well blended. Bring to a boil, reduce heat, cover and simmer for 2 to 2½ hours.

Strain soup. Place vegetables into food processor or blender and puree.

Mix cornstarch with remaining water and blend until smooth. Add to soup and cook 15 minutes, stirring, until stock is thickened. Add Worcestershire sauce and chopped parsley. Add meat and vegetable puree. Remove from direct heat.

Add sherry right before serving.

PART V

THE ORIGINALS

15

Sansom Street Oyster House (Original)

1516 Sansom Street

The history of Sansom Street Oyster House starts way before the current restaurant debuted in 2008—as far back as 1947. David Mink's father, Sam, purchased Kelly's on Mole Street in 1947—this was the year David was born, and his father's purchase was an oyster house legacy that was started in 1901 by Mary and "Pa" Kelly. In the late '60s, Sam had to close Kelly's—not because of sales, but because the entire Mole Street block was purchased for the future home of two office towers of Centre Square.

But the show must go on. Sam moved the *new* Kelly's to 1620 Ludlow Street and readied the space for its debut. Two months prior to launch, while David was studying at Cornell University, Sam died of a heart attack. His children, David and his sister, Nancy, decided to follow through on his wishes. David left school and opened the new-and-improved Kelly's in November 1969.

However, the brother-and-sister arrangement didn't last for long. Nancy left in May 1970, and the burden of the restaurant fell on the young twenty-three-year-old's shoulders, so David took a hiatus while his mother, Sylvia, continued to run the show. Eventually, in 1973, Sylvia sold Kelly's and its adjoining parking lot for $2.3 million.

Older, wiser and inspired now to follow in his father's footsteps, in 1976, David reemerged on the 1500 block of Sansom Street in a former cafeteria, looking to re-create the charm of Kelly's in his own way. Mink's personal touches stayed true to what Kelly's did best but elevated his oyster house to the modern day. He sourced unusual artisan cheeses from a farm in Vermont he liked to visit; he curated an elite loose-leaf tea and wine list and he even dressed the wall with the family's age-old glitzy oyster plate collection.

Business was so good that in 1981, Mink opened a second restaurant, Dockside Fish Company, at Eighth and Locust Streets. Eventually, that offshoot ran its course, closing in 1987. He didn't stop there. In 1989, while the oyster house continued with success, he opened the Sam Adams Brew House upstairs, the first-ever brewpub in Philadelphia, which was a 50-50 venture with Boston Brewing Company.

Mink said in their heyday, the two operations complemented each other, with the younger clientele going upstairs and the older focused on the enjoyment of oysters and wine. "Either place is unpretentious," relayed Mink, in 1997 to the *Inquirer*. "That's not what we're about. We're not a specialty-occasion restaurant. We were never considered part of the restaurant renaissance in Philadelphia because our formula was too traditional. But many of those other places are all gone and we're still around. We're like the tortoise and the hare."

"The triumph of Sansom Street's big transformations last August [came] from the ability to refine and modernize without compromising its identity, and it is a success in both look and flavor," wrote Craig LaBan in an early January 2000 restaurant review in the *Inquirer*.

Like the name assumed, the raw oyster experience was elevated above the rest. Sit at the bar and peer over at the shuckers, gracefully slicing your share of the best oysters in town. The space was quoted as "the place" for fresh, well-handled oysters year after year. Mink took pride in doing a lot of hands-on oyster prospecting, seeking out new varieties to delight patrons. Mink was known to suggest that you needed nothing more than a squirt of lemon and a dash of black pepper for a raw oyster to be enjoyable, encouraging folks to enjoy them at their purest, unadulterated, but cocktail sauce, horseradish and mignonette were available on hand.

Fried oysters and chicken salad were a classic Philadelphia oyster house combination dating back to the nineteenth century, and Sansom Street did it well, with oysters cloaked in a cornmeal crust and delightfully creamy inside. They also kept for years a crab imperial, which LaBan quoted was a "wonder of simple old-time richness," as dressed to the original Kelly's recipe of a creamy glaze of sherry, dry mustard and mayo.

Up until 2000, Sansom Street's desserts were crafted by what some called the city's most experienced active cook, eighty-six-year-old John Johnson, a veteran of Kelly's, who had worked for the Mink family since the '60s. His specialties marked unmistakable authenticity, such as hot apple brown betty and sweet potato pie.

In 2000, David Mink decided to sell the Sansom Street Oyster House to his then executive chef of two years, Cary Neff. (Neff previously owned a namesake restaurant around the corner.) Mink did, however, continue to own the bricks, while Neff owned the business.

Neff brought critical acclaim to the oyster house for his introduction of a daily selection of fresh fish, typically served with casual, non-fussy nods to Asian and contemporary flavors. He also introduced new varieties of oysters—including the lush Cape May Salts.

In 2007, Craig LaBan reported in the *Philadelphia Inquirer* that Neff's oyster house was the "best raw bar west of Broad Street." Around the same time, Neff opened another restaurant, Coquette Bistro & Raw Bar, at South Fifth Street.

In June 2008, after a thirty-two-year-stint, Sansom Street Oyster House closed its doors. Rick Nichols wrote then in his "On the Side" column in the *Inquirer* that it was a "determinedly Philadelphian fixture."

But, it wasn't closed for long. David Mink loves a good comeback, and he and his son Sam—like a young David, now interested in the family business—gave the restaurant a complete top-to-bottom makeover, including slicing the name to just "Oyster House." The restaurant reopened in June 2008. They continued to serve the classics (raw oysters, fried oysters and chicken salad) as well as some reinvented twists—a new school, no-roux snapper soup. While the reinvention did have a few more modern takes than previous iterations, including a premium twenty-six-dollar lobster roll built on a toasted bun sourced from Maine, many locals met the opening with delightful purrs of "our oyster house is alive again!"

Oyster House continues to live on with Sam Mink at the helm. Eventually, in the upstairs space that once held the Sam Adams' brewpub and after that Nodding Head Brewery, came Sam's hip, millennial-loved venture, Mission Taqueria.

Sansom Street Oyster House Recipe: Oyster Mignonette
Recipe dictated by Neff to *Journal News*, 2003

¼ cup shallots
2 tablespoons cracked black pepper

½ cup sugar
¾ cup red wine vinegar

Dice shallots and combine with the rest of the ingredients. Stir until the sugar dissolves. Spoon over raw oysters.

Sansom Street Oyster House Recipe: Oyster Stew
Recipe dictated by Neff to *Journal News*, 2003
I entrée serving or serves 2 as appetizer

6 small-to-medium oysters shucked (Box oysters, known also as Long Island Half Shells, recommended)
½ teaspoon Worcestershire sauce
Pinch Old Bay seasoning
I pat butter
2 cups half-and-half or milk

Combine the oysters and their liquor, Worcestershire, seasoning and butter. Simmer over medium heat for 2 minutes. Heat the cream separately. Pour the warmed oysters in a tureen and top with hot half-and-half or milk.

16

Friday Saturday Sunday (Original)

261 South Twenty-First Street

I t opened in 1973 during the war baby generation. *Philadelphia Magazine* said that when war babies discovered that there were "no places in the city to satisfy their budding gourmet lusts, they simply fell back on the tactics of participatory democracy and opened their own." Many of those sparked with the restaurant-owning bug would pool their money together, owning and operating an establishment collectively sometimes on a part-time basis. That's exactly how Friday Saturday Sunday came to be.

Former schoolteacher/dancer Tom Hunter was the only full-timer, with other partners including Jeanine Autret of the *Daily News*, advertiser Arnie Roberts, photographer Weaver Lilley, carpenter Bud Bretschneider, former psychologist Jay Gubin and, ironically, Anne Perrier, wife of Le Bec-Fin's Georges.

The name Friday Saturday Sunday was once referred to as the only three days of the week that this tiny restaurant was open for business. Later they added "Thursday Too" when they started to expand their hours. This was the early '70s, when Philadelphians were still being told they didn't go out to dinner, but when the partners learned that there was a local market for inventive cooking, they took it into their own hands and slowly expanded hours until they became open seven days a week.

Friday Saturday Sunday appealed to the young, affluent, artsy-type of diners, dressed with fancy drapes tenting the ceiling like an elaborate circus tent and giving a laid-back vibe. The setting was casual, with plasticized tables and green plants, and the owners encouraged you to bring your own wine—an uncommon bring-your-own ask at the time. (Over time, they secured a liquor license and built a reputation for some of the city's finest cocktails.)

At the restaurant's start, a diner could get a complete meal for $6.00. That was comparable to a cheap meal in Chinatown or South Philadelphia at the time. Madeira and pork-and-chicken-liver country pâté would cost you $1.25, with raw rockfish ceviche with pickled peppers and coriander the priciest appetizer at $1.50. Mousseline of flounder or curried chicken were popular entrées, and folks loved to gobble up the "Chili Elizabeth Taylor." For decades, the cognac-splashed mushroom soup with cream and Kennett Square mushrooms won critic's hearts, citing it as a "soup like no other" and "worth trying since you'll probably be craving it again."

The quality of the food attracted the same clientele who also celebrated Julia Child–type home cooking and appreciated a good Rittenhouse Square address. Diners never knew what they'd be surprised with when they arrived to order off of a chalked blackboard promoting Italian osso buco and some of the best desserts in town. The kitchen wasn't about producing the buzziest dishes but instead, busted out plates screaming with soul that stood the test of time.

In 2004, then *Philly Mag* food writer Emily Teel moved to an apartment right across the street from Friday Saturday Sunday. "The upstairs glowed blue.… Downstairs, a steady trickle of neighborhood regulars for whom the place was an institution, tucking into bowls of mushroom soup. Frankly, I never quite understood the appeal, but I learned a lot that year…and I understood the restaurant as a beloved institution in Philadelphia's dining scene."

Another *Philly Mag* writer, Trey Popp, featured the restaurant in his "Revisit" column in 2011. "The kitchen [was] three steps behind in trends anyway," but that wasn't what it was about. It focused on dishes from pork chops with whipped potatoes and Caesar salad to crab cakes with jicama slaw.

For four decades, Friday Saturday Sunday never took reservations but still remained successfully busy. It was one of the last remaining restaurants from Philadelphia's first restaurant renaissance and, as of 2015, the oldest restaurant in Center City.

This is where it gets interesting. In 2015, Chad and Hanna Williams, then working together at Amada, heard that Friday Saturday Sunday was quietly going up for sale. Hanna, having grown up in Philly and been a regular at the restaurant's upstairs Tank Bar (there was an illuminated 135-gallon fish tank in the bar, hence the name), encouraged her partner that they should buy the bricks from the original owners.

"My parents used to drink at this bar before I was born, so I understood what an institution it was," she told *Food & Wine* magazine in 2019. "I think we both saw the potential it had, if it was to be reinvented."

And so they did. The original proprietor Lilley cited in her August 2015 closing letter that they were an "exciting couple," but suggested "all things must come to an end" and "it had been [their] pleasure and honor to serve for the past 42 years."

Lilley threw a wine dinner to celebrate the end of the original Friday Saturday Sunday, which included chilled cucumber and yogurt soup with langoustine, torchon of foie gras with mustard seeds and figs, squid ink pasta with brandade, rack of lamb with huckleberry harissa and signature desserts.

The Williamses took over ownership as of August 2015 and spent eighteen months transforming it from its current state, which was last updated in the 1980s. The bi-level space was transformed with elegance and class, including flipping the Tank Bar into a vibrant upstairs dining room—which has an ornate golden cage on display, a homage to the coffee shop Gilded Cage, which predated the original Friday Saturday Sunday. Downstairs was flipped with a black-and-white-checkered floor and lined with a swanky marble bar that generously takes up the whole room.

Once the Williamses opened up their version of Friday Saturday Sunday in 2016, it reemerged and earned its rightful place back in the Philadelphia food scene, becoming one of the most dynamic and respected restaurants.

Nowadays, the restaurant is opened five days a week (Wednesday through Saturday) and draws crowds of both former regulars and pretty much any other Philadelphian eager to score a reservation. For a while, the bar opened at three o'clock—a carryover from back in the day—which hadn't stopped anyone. Those seats are still hard to come by.

Friday Saturday Sunday Recipe: Cream of Mushroom Soup
The original Friday Saturday Sunday recipe
Serves 6

1 pound portabella mushrooms or 1 pound oyster mushrooms
¼ cup butter
2 tablespoons flour
1 quart chicken stock

1 quart heavy cream
Cognac, to taste
Salt, white pepper, to taste

Chop mushrooms into a fine dice. Place in a large sauce pot with the butter, and sauté until most of the liquid in the mushrooms is cooked off. Sprinkle flour over the mushroom mixture.

Stir while cooking for a few minutes, then add chicken stock and mix well. Allow mixture to reduce over a medium flame to half its original volume (about 30 minutes). Refrigerate until just before dinner.

Before serving, heat mixture while adding heavy cream. Add cognac and salt and white pepper to taste.

PART VI

MEMORABLE RESTAURATEURS
WHO SET A NEW CULINARY PACE

17
In Season

315 South Thirteenth Street

In 1976, then twenty-eight-year-old Cheltenham, Pennsylvania resident Andrew Schloss enrolled in the Restaurant School in Center City. Two days after graduation, he and fellow student Ken Silveri decided to open their own restaurant, In Season, at Thirteenth and Pine Streets. Together, they transformed the former Gilded Cage, a dark and smoky coffee shop for folk singers and beatniks of another era, into an all-American eatery that concentrated on fresh and natural foods. (Schloss himself had dreams of opening a Japanese restaurant, Silveri dreams of an Italian establishment. The fresh food–focused In Season was a restaurant concept that satisfied both aspiring restaurateurs.) Opening day was July 7, 1977.

In Season customers didn't need a calendar to know the time of year. If there were lots of cold platters of fresh fish, fruit desserts and local vegetables on the menu, it must have been summer. Fall signaled turkey sautéed in vermouth with oysters and local mushrooms or sausage, sweet potato and apricot stew. In spring, you'd find artichokes stuffed with ricotta cheese and pesto or leek and rabbit pie. Presentation was as important as the seasonality of the ingredients.

Built in a long, narrow room customized by master architect James Kruly close to the Academy of Music, the co-chefs and owners constructed In Season's reputation around their notions of celebrating creative food built with seasonal ingredients. The menu appealed to meat-and-potato eaters as it did more adventurous diners. The co-owners saw diners wanting lighter, less "prepared" foods that maintained the integrity of the ingredients. Most fruits and vegetables served at In Season were as natural as possible, including raw or close to it.

The youthful proprietors said their goal was to offer foods that were visually exciting, nutritionally sound and affordable. The popularity of the small, highly personal restaurant indicated they met their goal. "I was into health foods for a while, but I don't cook just for vitamin content. The sensuality of food must not be cut," Schloss told *Courier-Post* at the height of In Season's success.

For five years, the owners would produce new menus four times a year, requiring month-long research leading up to the new menu's debut. They'd explore peak ripeness and in-season quality of their to-be-featured ingredients and also review new inventive techniques and ways to vary the in-season foodstuffs. Sometimes, they'd even evaluate more than two hundred recipes that could be featured until they narrowed down to a doable two dozen that would be possible to execute out of the small In Season kitchen.

Baking was done on the premises, and desserts included the restaurant's raved twelve-hour cream cheesecake or the fruity froths the owners called "clouds." (The owners justified desserts by calling them good for your mental health.)

The trend-conscious In Season was apropos for its time, instrumental in pushing Philadelphia's dining scene renaissance and educating diners about the importance of the in-season quality for produce well before "farm to table" dining was cool. Unique as In Season was, the restaurant eventually struggled with turning a profit, citing inflation and a less-than-ideal location. The restaurant, however, didn't give up without a fight. During the continued restaurant boom in the mid-'80s, Silveri reconceptualized the restaurant to be more approachable to everyday diners. They went from serving costly American cuisine to inexpensive pasta and burgers. With In Season, he and his partners decided they couldn't survive on serving baked quail and venison filets alone.

"We were much more interested in being creative, inventive and making a statement than being businessmen," Silveri told the *Inquirer* in 1984, during the time the restaurant pivoted. "There was no steak. There was never anything plain, and that limited our market."

If the city was starving for gourmet restaurants then, In Season as conceived may have lived on for many years. "When we opened in 1977, we were one of the few," Silveri continued. "When we closed, we were one of many and we were all competing for the same customer."

Following the closing of In Season, Silveri reframed the concept into a namesake restaurant that specialized in buffalo wings (he is a native of Buffalo, New York, after all) and was a place where a couple could buy a dinner for twelve dollars. Schloss, no longer a partner, stayed in the kitchen for some time until he went on to work as the culinary director of the Restaurant School of Philadelphia. He reported that he preferred cooking and teaching to the hassles of owning a business. Additionally, he regularly contributed to the food section of the *Inquirer* and continues to publish a wide range of culinary cookbooks, including *Cooking Slow: Recipes for Slowing Down and Cooking More.*

In Season Recipe: Eggplant Caviar
Adapted from the *Philadelphia Inquirer*, 1978
Serves 4–6

1 eggplant
¼ cup olive oil
2 cloves garlic, crushed
1 sweet red pepper, chopped
¼ cup capers
¼ cup red wine vinegar
Juice of a ½ lemon
1 tablespoon marjoram
Dash hot sauce
Salt, pepper
2 tomatoes, chopped

Peel and chop eggplant in half-inch cubes. Macerate by sprinkling with salt and letting stand 15 minutes to extract liquid. Rinse and drain on paper towels.

Heat oil in heavy sauté pan. Sauté onion and garlic until soft; add red pepper and eggplant. Cook until just barely tender. Add capers, wine vinegar, lemon juice, marjoram, hot pepper sauce, salt and pepper. Bring to boiling and remove from heat.

Add tomatoes. Chill. Serve cold.

18

James

824 South Eighth Street

If the name Jim Burke rings a bell, it tells a lot about where you were in 2007 and if you were in touch with the thriving Philadelphia restaurant scene. Then, alongside his wife and business partner, Kristina, he was running one of the city's most promising restaurants, James, named after himself.

James, gracefully nestled in the Bella Vista neighborhood, was known for its romantic ambiance and excellent contemporary American menu with elegant Northern Italian influences based on locally grown seasonal ingredients. Before opening James with Kristina, Burke worked with top chefs—as Marc Vetri's sous chef at Vetri and with Vince Alberici of The Marker. He later headed the kitchen at Stephen Starr's Angelina. He also did a stint at the Michelin-starred Ristorante Frosio in Almè, Italy.

James was a pleasant city hideaway, able to accommodate sixty for dinner and twenty at its bar, and during winter, it roared with a glowing fireplace.

As *Philadelphia City Paper* said, "There's no such thing as a perfect restaurant, but James comes awfully close for a chef making his first real step out on his own." On top of that, Jim was *really nice*. Locals found pride in supporting him.

His tasting menu may have been a splurge, ranging from five to nine courses, but it was worth every penny to allow your taste buds to dance through selections like risotto alla Milanese with summer truffles; wild king salmon with potatoes rösti and caviar sauce; and roast of Jamison Farm lamb crowned with baby carrots, leeks and fennel jus. There might have been showstoppers like the hand-cut pappardelle duck ragout dressed with orange zest and bittersweet chocolate—which was the one dish that *never* left the menu—or the delicate risi e bisi, which was a risotto with mint, peas and a bacon-infused gelato, as well as the risotto named after Jim's wife, alla Kristina, that was soaked in prosecco and oysters. Of course, dessert was equally promising, with sweet endings like the gingered rhubarb sugar triangle topped with honey cream that tasted like summer itself.

And the well-versed front of the house—thanks to Kristina—brought the elaborate, yet comforting experience to life, spouting the term *umami* about this dish like it was common speak (which, in 2007, was only for the most-educated foodies). There was also a smart Eurocentric wine list to round out your experience and notable herb-infused cocktails.

James was a critic's paradise, achieving recognition on a regional and national level. The *Philadelphia Inquirer* gave it a glowing three-bell review, claiming it was "one of the most exciting new restaurants" its opening year, relaying that its success was attributed to "its palpable personal style and fine-dining passion, and a crisp contemporary vision for how the best ingredients can be shaped by authentic Italian inspirations."

Food & Wine magazine named Burke the Best New Chef of 2008; he received semifinalist nominations for a James Beard Award for three years running, 2008, 2009 and 2010; and the restaurant was a finalist for Bocuse d'Or USA 2010.

Philadelphia food critic Adam Erace wrote that James served "the kind of food we take for granted now but was completely uncommon when they opened in 2006."

But all the accolades don't guarantee success. "We got hit really hard by the economic downturn, being a fine dining restaurant," relayed Burke. In 2011, he and his wife decided not to renew James's lease, which was something Kristina described to a reporter as "heartbreaking."

When Jim and Kristina Burke closed James in 2011 and decamped to NYC, wails of unhappiness echoed through the Philly food community. After James, Burke was granted the opportunity to team up with Stephen Starr again to open Caffe Storico in New York. Jim recognized the importance of cooking in one of the greatest food cities and jumped at the chance. He breathed fresh life into the renovated property and infused his modern take on *cichetti* (i.e., Venetian-style small plates) and an array of handmade pastas.

Eventually, Burke went on to cook for Daniel Boulud at Bistro Moderne. He returned "home" to Philadelphia in 2014 to be an instructor for Drexel University's hospitality program, consult with restaurants like Tredici and Pizzeria Felici and develop the brewhouse menu at Yards' Spring Garden location. He also did a stint as the chef in residence at Morgan's Pier in 2016. In late 2019, he made his triumphant return to fine dining, taking over as executive chef at Wm. Mulherin's in the Fishtown neighborhood.

19

Django

526 South Fourth Street

Before there was Aimee Olexy and Stephen Starr, one of the city's most successful restaurant partnerships, there was Aimee Olexy and Bryan Sikora (chef and Olexy's then husband). Django's homespun chic vibe and killer cheese plate signaled what was to come. Both Olexy and Sikora have since gone on to better things: he owns concepts in Wilmington and Kennett Square, and she's become an iconic restaurateur in Philly.

Starr had been a fan of Amy's since 1999, when she launched and managed the Blue Angel, his late French bistro on Chestnut Street. "I was struck by her intelligence," he recalled. When Olexy left Starr in 2001 to open Django, the Blue Angel lost its focus and customers, closing in 2003.

Working for Starr—Amy as the director of restaurants and Bryan as Tangerine's chef—was enough to convince them that the corporate world was too large.

May 2001 marked Olexy's true arrival onto the Philadelphia restaurateur scene. That March, she and Bryan Sikora debuted Django, the Society Hill restaurant that's still, to this day, the only BYOB eatery ever to earn a four-bell rating from *Philadelphia Inquirer* critic Craig LaBan. Unforgettably, he wrote that Django "manages to communicate—without the usual public-relations pyrotechnics—the heart and polish that make a restaurant great." The couple wanted a "personal" and "food-driven" restaurant, and they succeeded by developing what may be the hottest ticket in town.

On LaBan's inexact scale, food, service and ambiance are weighed with longevity. Netting four bells typically takes at least two years, which is all Django needed to become the first and only BYO to be so honored. "Craig gave it the most gushing review in restaurant history," says Starr, with more than a hint of envy. *Gourmet* magazine named Django one of the one hundred finest restaurants in the country. The wait for a reservation was eight weeks.

Django charmed with flowerpots of fresh-baked bread, signature Highfield Dairy goat cheese gnocchi and juicy whole roasted quail, fat with a bread and giblet stuffing.

Reviewers ran out of superlatives. *New York Times* writer Regina Schrambling wrote, "[Django] is a personal statement that the reinvention of crème brûlée as a napoleon is a goal more worthy than fine linens and the ultimate wine cellar."

"I knew Django was special immediately," Olexy said of the tiny thirty-eight-seat restaurant, where she was a constant front-of-house presence. She still remembers her first customer. "He was telling me how much he loved cheese, and I felt the glimmer of hope," the restaurateur recalled. "And he said he loved fish soup. I said, 'Come tomorrow.' He did, and we had it ready for him."

Django was synonymous with outstanding seasonal cuisine that credited local farms on the menu, gracious service and sweet surroundings since the little storefront opened, one of the first of the still-going-strong BYOB boom. (From the start, the couple didn't want to tie up space and money with a wine cellar.) All who loved the original restaurant agreed that Sikora and Olexy would be a tough act to follow. The ever-evolving menu was anything but predictable, and on a given night you might find yourself having to make the tough but rewarding choice between the familiar (perhaps a well-conceived roasted duck or veal sirloin) and something a touch more exotic, like grilled octopus or venison with mole. There was always a famed cheese plate.

In 2005, to the shock of some, Olexy and Sikora decided to sell Django at the height of its popularity and relocate to Pennsylvania's Chester County, where in 2007 they opened Talula's Table. The "Talula" part was in honor of their daughter, Annalee Talula Rae. The "Table" part, meanwhile, referred to the gourmet market by day's nightly twelve-person BYOB tastings, so incredibly coveted that reservations had to be made a full calendar year in advance. Portfolio.com dubbed it "The Toughest Table in America." The *New York Times* praised the "handsome, deceptively complex and masterfully executed" food, likening the experience to a "spiritual retreat." The experience earned a spot on the 2010 *Saveur* 100 list, which informed us that "the magic has to do with more than just the menu—it's the sense of community."

Django did experience a short-lived three-year revival under the new ownership of Greg Salisbury and chef Ross Essner. While the revival was positioned as a more rustic neighborhood bistro and casual attempt at a restaurant of the same name, it never quite reached the four-bell recognition that its former superstar owners received. "The old Django didn't earn four bells because of its cozy setting, or because it was an iconic BYO," wrote Laban. "Sikora's cooking was simply that good—intensely seasonal, uniquely inventive, and flawlessly done."

Django Recipe: Spiced Red Tail Venison Carpaccio, White Runner Bean Puree, Parmesan Socca Cracker, Truffle Vinaigrette
Adapted by StarChefs
Serves 6

Venison
1 loin venison, 6–8 ounces, trimmed and tied
Salt, pepper
3 star anise, ground
10 fennel seeds, ground
Peanut oil

Socca
2 ounces chickpea flour
1 tablespoon Parmesan cheese
1 tablespoon olive oil
3–4 ounces water
Salt

Black Truffle Juice
6 ounces black truffle juice
1–2 teaspoon cornstarch

Runner Bean Puree
8 ounces French runner beans, soaked overnight
1 large carrot, cut into thirds
1 onion, split
1 celery stalk, cut into thirds
1 fresh bay leaf
1 teaspoon black truffle oil
3 ounces olive oil
2 ounces Parmesan cheese

Vinaigrette
2 shallots, minced, sautéed and cooled
1 ounce champagne vinegar
1 ounce sherry vinegar
½ teaspoon salt
3–4 ounces olive oil
6 ounces black truffle juice, thickened
1 tablespoon finely chopped thyme
1 tablespoon finely chopped rosemary
1 tablespoon finely chopped parsley

Petite Garnish Salad
Chiffonade of radicchio, about four leaves
Frisée leaves (tender center)

For Venison
Season venison generously with salt and pepper and rub meat with ground spices. Heat a large sauté pan with enough peanut oil to thickly coat pan. Once pan begins to smoke, gently place meat in pan. Sear meat on all sides. Remove venison and cool on rack to room temperature. Wrap venison in plastic and freeze until firm.

When ready to serve, remove venison from freezer and allow it to sit at room temperature for 15–20 minutes. If the meat is too cold, it will crumble. Slice venison across the grain, as thinly as possible, using a meat slicer or a very sharp kitchen knife.

For Socca
Puree chickpea flour, Parmesan, olive oil and water together in blender until smooth. Add salt to taste. Cook the socca like a crepe over low

even heat in a nonstick pan with nonstick spray oil. Once edges begin to turn brown, the socca should begin to release itself. Keep socca in a 100-degree oven until ready to use.

For Black Truffle Juice

In a small saucepan, heat truffle juice and cornstarch over low flame. Modify amount of cornstarch depending on preference of sauce consistency.

For Runner Bean Puree

Place beans in a large pot with carrot, split onion, celery, bay leaf. Add enough water to cover beans. Cook until tender over medium-high heat. Remove vegetables and bay leaf and drain, reserving liquid. Puree runner beans in a food processor with black truffle oil, olive oil and Parmesan cheese until smooth. Use reserved bean liquid to adjust consistency so it is smooth but not runny.

For Herb Oil

Puree all ingredients in food processor until smooth. Allow mixture to infuse for one hour and then pass through a fine sieve.

For Vinaigrette

Puree sautéed shallots and both vinegars in a blender. Add salt and olive oil, blending to emulsify. Next blend in thickened truffle juice and transfer vinaigrette to a storage container. Stir in chopped herbs and reserve.

To Serve

Arrange six to eight slices of venison on a plate and dress liberally with vinaigrette. Dress petite greens with vinaigrette in a bowl; put a dollop of bean puree in the center of plated venison slices and top with socca. Place a tangle of the dressed petite salad on top of the socca. Finish with a drizzle of herb oil, a sprinkling of sea salt and a dusting of finely grated Parmesan cheese.

20

Koo Zee Doo

614 North Second Street

Prior to the introduction of Koo Zee Doo to Philadelphia's Northern Liberties neighborhood, Philadelphians with a hankering for Portuguese cuisine would have to travel to New Jersey or the Northeast. Koo Zee Doo was short-lived, but special, with its three-year stint from 2009 to 2013. A husband-and-wife team, chef and James Beard Award winner David Gilberg and pastry chef Carla Goncalves, filled in the local void with a culinary passion that elevated the rustic flavors of Portugal to rare sophistication.

The restaurant's name was derived from the phonetic spelling of both *cozhinado*, the Portuguese word for "cooked," and Cozido a Portuguesa, a traditional Portuguese dish.

It celebrated Goncalves's heritage through a menu based off of her family's recipes and dishes you would have found served at her home in northern Portugal. The inspired family-style dishes were even served in traditional Portuguese pottery to bring the experience full circle.

Many of the products rounding out the menu, such as olive oil and sea salt, were imported from Portugal. The chef had a local New Jersey source for his chorizo and other sustainable, fresh meats he served on his menu.

Inquirer's Craig LaBan wrote in his excellent three-bell review that the BYOB exuded "unabashed zest of pure Portuguese soul." The critic also relayed that Koo Zee Doo was the first kitchen he'd experienced in the States that elevated the authentic flavors of Portugal to another level.

The husband and wife were capable of embracing rustic food for pure grace, managing to turn chicken gizzards into a best-seller. (Their interpretation was milk-soaked and then braised with wine and a garlicky *refogado* that turned them into dark meat nuggets.) Gilberg didn't outsmart Portuguese cuisine in modern executions but instead celebrated their simplicity and enhanced their foundation through high-quality, in-season ingredients and pinch-perfect techniques.

Each dish was a gem of refined authenticity: from homemade breads like the earthy *broa de milho* made of cornmeal and flour; to the baked duck rice with chorizo, whole grilled sardines and tuna-stuffed turnovers; and soulful soups like the *caldo verde* (a recipe from Carla's mother) and *acorda de cogumelos* (bread soup); family-style entrées like the *carne de porco a Alentenjano*, a wholesome mix of pork and clams, or the local rabbit stewed "hunter-style." Add in warm service and a flickering candlelit romance, and Northern Liberties had a charming new winner.

Of course, Goncalves's sweet endings were not to be missed either. One of the most delightfully rich coconut desserts in the city was her moist shredded coconut tart layered with yolk-enriched syrup. The chocolate "salami," a rolled ganache with crushed cookies sliced from a tube, and the chestnut-stuffed and chocolate-covered figs from the *prato de chocolate* were memorable meal-enders, as was the *pastel de nata*, a traditional tart that is rich in egg custard.

The exposed-brick location, which was once occupied by the likes of Copper Bistro and Aden, provided an appropriate backdrop to the comforting menu, with its warmth coming from simple, wall-hung flickering votives, an unpretentious wide-open kitchen that was steps away from the front-room diners, cork-topped tables and a *Gallo de Barcelos* rooster painted on the wall for good luck. Young servers buzzed around in casual, comfortable dress: simple black T-shirts and jeans.

And good luck was had. Critics praised Koo Zee Doo, including a *Philadelphia Magazine* nod for "best restaurant."

Gilberg's fiery *piri* hot sauce even became so popular that he began bottling it in 2012 for those who cared to take the inferno on the road. Made with dried malagueta peppers, garlic sea salt and vinegar, the pale orange sauce had a sharp, fruity heat and a leveled tang.

Slow weeknights eventually prompted Gilberg and Goncalves to close down their memorable BYOB when their lease was up on July 14, 2013. Koo Zee Doo did a good thing for Philadelphia in its short stint, but there continues to be a Portuguese void.

A year later, in the summer of 2014, Gilberg reappeared as the chef in residence at Morgan's Pier. Then, in early 2019, they resurfaced with a new concept, Cry Baby Pasta, a joint venture with another restaurant couple, Bridget Foy and Paul Rodriguez. Filling a storied Queen Village space that once housed Judy's Café, Ansill and Ela, the restaurant specializes in fresh pastas, bruschetta and family-style Italian entrées. If you're lucky, they will host another nostalgia-ridden Koo Zee Doo pop-up meal at Cry Baby, as they did in late 2019.

21

Pif & Ansill

Pif: 1009 South Eighth Street
Ansill: 627 South Third Street

David Ansill had a multidecade Philly career. He was—and continues to be—a Philadelphia legend, raised in the Cheltenham neighborhood and trained at Philadelphia's Restaurant School in the late '80s. He never strayed too far from his home turf—well, besides the times he took off for warmer weather to Miami and later Jamaica.

To understand his restaurants, you should first understand how he got his start. Prior to going to culinary school, he kickstarted his time in the restaurant scene in 1976 by bar-backing at Grendel's Lair on South Street, a live music venue that was famous for the production of *Let My People Come*. Post his culinary education, he bounced around several local institutions, like Serrano's, The Bank, Treetops at the Rittenhouse Hotel—which has since evolved into Lacroix—and Judy's. He temporarily flew the coop to Miami, but after a few months, restaurateur Stephen Starr summoned him back home to work on a new concept, which became The Continental.

While Ansill helped to make The Continental a smash hit as the sous chef, he and Starr didn't see eye to eye. In true Ansill fashion, he couldn't stay there forever and eventually moved across the street to work at Lucy's Hat Shop. In the kitchen at Lucy's was where he developed the idea for his first restaurant, Pif.

"It was the late '90s and Philly was still in cheesesteak mode, and I wanted to do French peasant bistro food in a town that hadn't really seen it yet," said

Ansill to *Philadelphia Eater*'s critic Collin Flatt. "Pif was my baby. It still is." It opened on July 17, 2001, at Eighth and Carpenter Streets.

At Pif, Ansill quickly became known for signature dishes like his steak tartare with purple mustard, cognac and fried capers; stuffed pigs' feet; and the way-ahead-of-its-time sea urchin toast. He was daring in the kitchen and became a critic wunderkind, delighting senses with every last bite.

"David was always five years ahead of the curve, using ingredients people weren't ready for, or thought they weren't ready for," said *Inquirer* critic Craig LaBan to *Eater*. "Here was this journeyman chef that ended up achieving more than anyone could ever dream. He was an icon to the BYOB movement and developed sophisticated cuisine we had yet to experience."

"Before any trip I would take on a plane, I ate at Pif the night before," said *Philadelphia Magazine* food critic Joy Manning. "You know, in case the plane crashed. I always wanted it to be my last meal. It was the first place I ate escargot. His use of lavender stays with me to this day."

Without skipping a beat and because Pif business was booming, Ansill opened his larger and more expensive namesake restaurant at Third and Bainbridge Streets.

Though, with more restricting overhead than Pif, he eventually closed Ansill to reset and reconvert Ansill into Ansill Food + Wine. Here, he was quickly pigeonholed as the chef that served "all offal, all the time." "I think it's funny, the menu was largely like Pif, but I got labeled the 'weird food' guy. That killed us," said Ansill.

Sure, he laid claim to interesting ingredients to steal a dish's show, like crispy sweetbreads tumbled with fava beans and morels or quail marinated in balsamic. If his porky renditions of daring ingredients did well, he wasn't a one-trick pony. He delighted guests with cheese and charcuterie boards layered with nutty Idiazabal, house-made quince paste and house-cured duck prosciutto. He had vegetarian favorites like cool mint- and yogurt-infused pea soup and porcini mushrooms sautéed with taleggio cheese.

Desserts were thanks to his wife, Catherine Gilbert-Ansill, serving mesmerizing red wine syrup–soaked saffron cheesecake and bee pollen–dressed panna cotta.

Eventually, Ansill and Pif closed, and Ansill took a couple of years off, reemerging later at the Ladder 15. Giving the party bar a culinary reputation for two years, he brought back a Pif-themed tasting menu on Tuesdays to showcase the notable dishes to a new audience. He introduced a buzzy burger that was served with a large chunk of bone marrow that diners loved to scoop out and brag to all their foodie friends about.

Always full of surprises, Ansill, at the age of fifty-three, announced in January 2012 that he was bidding the city farewell to take up a chef residency in Jamaica at Bombay-born Toral Chudasama's Wild Parrot Guest Cottages' restaurant, Buddy's Beach Bar & Café. At the time, Ansill confessed to *Philadelphia Magazine* that he reached the end of his Philadelphia career. "What else am I going to do here?" he questioned. "I like to smoke pot. And I need to go somewhere that I can do that."

Ansill can never get enough of Philadelphia, though. He returned in 2013, showing up at Bar Ferdinand, garnering more rave reviews. Next on his tour was the Good King Tavern and then consulting at Washington West newcomer Pinefish. Around August 2016, he exited Pinefish and went silent—but only for a few months. At the end of the year, he resurfaced, announcing Pot Luck, an underground weed-infused dinner that would run monthly and cost diners one hundred dollars per person. (To make it not illegal you paid for the dinner, and the weed was basically free.) The menus would dance with dishes like marijuana-infused chile oil on salmon tartare; bone marrow whipped with ganja butter, spread across crostini placed in a bowl of truffle mushroom soup; tomato coulis with herb butter melted into it, swirled around a semolina goat cheese dumpling; and grilled marinated quail glazed with "medicated" Jamaican rum (a syrup based on a weed tincture of French *mirabelle eau de vie*, drizzled over a *marquise de chocolat*—a dish Ansill described as "basically chocolate butter").

He also came back for a one-night-only pop-up at Amis & M Restaurant, serving dishes that were iconic from his days at Pif, like the Escargot au Pif, steak tartare and smoked sausage and duck confit cassoulet.

When speaking to his legacy, he told *Eater*: "Cook the food you want, and trust your customers. Ultimately, love what you do in the kitchen. Sometimes it works, sometimes it doesn't. You don't have to be an asshole to be a chef. It's just food."

David Ansill Recipe: Paella
Adapted from the *Philadelphia Inquirer*, 2014
Makes 6 entrée servings

2 tablespoons olive oil
½ pound chorizo, sliced thin

½ pound boneless skinless chicken thighs, cut into bite-size pieces
2 small onions, diced
4 garlic cloves, minced
2 medium tomatoes, diced
1 cup bomba, calasparra, Arborio or Goya short-grain rice
3 cups chicken stock, heated (you might not need all of it)
3 grams Spanish saffron
12 littleneck clams
12 mussels
½ pound shrimp, cleaned
A couple of handfuls of haricots verts or peas
½ cup piquillo peppers, cut into thin strips

Heat oil in a 17-inch paella pan or cast-iron pan over medium-high heat. Sauté chorizo until brown, then remove and reserve. Add chicken to the pan and brown on all sides. Remove from pan and reserve.

In the same pan, make a sofrito by sautéing the onions and garlic until soft, being careful not to burn the garlic. Cook for 2 or 3 minutes on medium heat. Then add tomatoes and cook until the mixture caramelizes a bit and the ingredients become a thick, chunky sauce.

Fold in rice and stir-fry to coat the grains for 2 to 3 minutes, until the grains of rice turn opaque. Pour in ½ cup heated stock and let rice absorb almost all of the stock. Add saffron, stirring for the final time. Add clams, tucking them into the rice, and another ½ cup of heated stock. Cover. When stock is absorbed, add the mussels and another ¼ cup stock to the pan. Cover and let rice absorb stock. Add shrimp, chicken and chorizo and ½ cup stock. Cover and let rice absorb stock. Continue to add more stock in ½ cup increments if rice is still not cooked. If it seems tender, add haricot verts and/or peas and piquillo peppers/roasted peppers. Turn heat down to low, cover and let stand until all stock is absorbed and seafood has finished cooking.

To create the soccarat, the caramelized, crispy layer on the bottom of the pan, briefly turn up the heat to medium high and check after about a minute and a half, allowing the rice to crisp just enough, but not so much that it burns.

22

Marigold Kitchen

501 South Forty-Fifth Street, West Philadelphia

In mid-October 2004, chef-owner Steven Cook introduced a forty-six-seat, molecular gastronomy–focused BYOB in the culinary outskirts of West Philadelphia in a former boardinghouse. (Yes, that Steve Cook, who is one-half of the CookSolo duo behind the likes of Zahav.) It was situated in a storied Victorian rowhouse that sprang from the site of the former comfort-food haven Marigold Dining Room, and before that, the location dated back to 1934, with Marigold Tea Room. A copper-plated door met you on your arrival, and once you stepped inside into an enclosed porch, you heard fire crackling in the background.

It was the perfect escape from the hustle and bustle of Center City dining. It had sophisticated-meets-creative edge in comparison to other BYOs of its time. It became known through its fifteen-year stint as a talent-stretching incubator for local young chefs peddling to push culinary boundaries. Most notably, the kitchen—which became known as a "laboratory of modernist cooking"—put out some of the city's greatest restaurant talents: Jonathan Adams (co-owner of Rival Bros. Coffee), Erin O'Shea and, of course, Michael Solomonov (other half of CookSolo) and Steve Cook.

Cook, a thirty-one-year-old investment banker turned chef and son of a rabbi, previously worked at the now-closed Salt in Rittenhouse Square, under the culinary guide of chef Vernon Morales. Salt was notorious for stretching its molecular gastronomy into culinary techniques such as foam, and Marigold Kitchen followed suit. (Much of the Salt staff joined Cook at Marigold Kitchen.)

Here, Cook served what Craig LaBan reported in 2005 in the *Philadelphia Inquirer* as "one of the best pork chops [he had] ever tasted," pontificating that Cook had taken artful cues from re-creating a deconstructed Cuban sandwich to create the freestyle rendition: pork chops crusted with mustard seeds, served with a terrine of shaved potatoes layered with crisp Serrano ham and a Dijon-infused pork jus speckled with tiny cornichon pickle chips.

Fish, though, was said to be Cook's greatest talent, executing vibrantly unique dishes of butterfish over celery root puree with a petite shrimp roll steamed in a banana leaf and his roasted cod draped over cabbage, hedgehog mushrooms and a sea of urchin cream.

Seafood-focused dishes and the intricacies of each plate helped to push Marigold into a special occasion spot for well-coiffed University City students, attractive for its ever-evolving menu always bursting with new, experimental gastronomic tricks.

In 2006, Marigold Kitchen's name became associated with the same circles as Django once had, local critics scribing sentiments such as "is this avant-garde BYOB the next Django?"

In a few short years, Cook ceded his place in the kitchen to rising star and friend Michael Solomonov, and then in the fall of 2008, Erin O'Shea joined the culinary team as chef de cuisine. O'Shea joined after Michael Solomonov left his Mediterranean handprint on Marigold's menu. O'Shea was encouraged to do the same and make her own personal statement against the Marigold menu. Though she came from the southern age of cream-heavy kitchens, her cuisine meshed well with Solomonov's Mediterranean palette—preserved lemon, olive oil, parsley—and helped shape Marigold into its new age.

During O'Shea leadership over the kitchen, the menu also experienced significant price drops, which painted its desire to become a neighborhood destination again. Eventually, Cook and Solomonov handed off Marigold's day-to-day operations to O'Shea to focus their attention on their new, larger project: an Israeli restaurant at St. James Place, Zahav, that would quickly become the city's darling—and continues to be to the present day.

In late 2009, then thirty-three-year-old Villanova native Robert Halpern bought Marigold Kitchen from Cook and became the new executive chef. (O'Shea went to run the now-closed Percy Street Barbecue on South Street, a restaurant under Cook-Solo's restaurant family.)

Halpern continued the unique charm of Marigold, where the kitchen was known for its ability to push culinary boundaries through scientific techniques to ultimately reimagine the food you were about to enjoy.

Chefs Andrew Kochan and Tim Lanza took over ownership of the esteemed Marigold Kitchen in 2014, running the West Philadelphia restaurant until its close in 2019. *Courtesy of Dallyn Pavey.*

There were plenty of syringes, foaming canisters and quick-freeze liquid nitrogen tanks lining the kitchen, all in pursuit of deconstructing and reinventing a new dining experience with vapors, spheres, foams, gels and freeze-dried delights.

Robert Halpern first started the BYOB's legendary thirteen-to-sixteen-course tasting menus in 2009, at the height of the worldwide molecular gastronomy revolution. He valued fluidity when it came to seasonal cooking, introducing new dishes once the season and its produce provoked the change.

Eventually, in early 2014, Halpern enforced a "no menu" policy, which required the diner to have an open mind. In coming to the restaurant, you were buying into the two-hour tasting menu of sixteen elaborate, cutting-edge small plates. He and his team dazzled with gazpacho "dippin' dots," fingerling potato skins topped with Cheddar foam, liquid squash ravioli with banana salt and hamachi with mushroom dashi and a mushroom "forest."

Then, in June 2014, Halpern—after earning a three-bell review from the *Philadelphia Inquirer*—sold the restaurant to his two chef protégés, Andrew Kochan and Tim Lanza. (Halpern's third sous chef, Keith Krajewski, went on to open the hyped sandwich shop Middle Child.) The duo carried the kitchen's modernist torch onward with inventive multicourse tasting menus until they brought on Eric Leveillee as executive chef. With the help of his sous chef Kieran O'Sullivan and Kevin McWilliams, the three were able to push the restaurant in new, free-thinking ways and landed the restaurant back onto *Philadelphia Magazine*'s 50 Best Restaurants list. (Marigold Kitchen was known to have a shocking number of chefs in the kitchen, at times up to ten, plating nearly eight hundred small plates on a busy Saturday night.)

Leveillee, taking a cue from the legendary Copenhagen restaurant Noma, left his mark through inventive dishes; he toasted hay—for extracting flavor, of course—pureed fermented rice, froze buttermilk into granita and pureed it with oysters for one hell of a crudo and even transformed *rømmegrøt*, a rich porridge, to a sliced, fried handheld bite.

Lanza and Kochan continued their Marigold Kitchen success over to a second restaurant in 2018—a short-run Rittenhouse restaurant, TALK. Due to the financial problems stemming from TALK, the partners ultimately decided to close both Marigold Kitchen and TALK in early 2019. Chef Eric Leveillee went on to a high-profile job at Lacroix Restaurant at the Rittenhouse. The acclaimed West Philly rowhouse eventually went up for sale for $745,000 following the closure.

23

¡Pasión!

Argentinian Guillermo Pernot became a chef in 1991, but he got his start as a busboy turned waiter. He came to America in 1975 after being drafted by the Argentine army because he did not want to go. He first enrolled in Columbia University, and then, three years later, came to Philadelphia. Here he got his first job as a busboy at Fiddler, which was then Metropolis. Eventually, he went on to Neil Stein's Fish Market, La Panetiere, Downey's and Apropos. He even clocked a waiter stint at the Four Seasons' Fountain dining room, which he credits to teaching him a lot, before leaving the front of house to get behind the stove.

Earning his place in the kitchen, Pernot set off on his own in partnership with restaurant lifer and former Susanna Foo GM Michael Dombkoski. Together, in 1998, they introduced a Nuevo Latino restaurant, ¡Pasión!, to Philadelphia's Restaurant Row on Fifteenth Street. It was a testament to the chef's native cuisine that he planned to bring to the highest level of creative contemporary cooking and ultimately succeeded in raising it to an art form.

¡Pasión!'s theatrical menu connected to Pernot's Argentine roots with dishes such as ceviche, smoked rib-eye served with *moros y cristianos* (black beans and rice) and the iconic *parrillada mista*, an Argentinean mixed grill for two with lamb, two types of sausage (including a raisin-and-walnut blood sausage), short ribs and sirloin tips served in a custom-made ox-shaped hibachi. He specialized in serving Argentinian beef, which he relayed was "very intense. In Argentina, cattle are raised on alfalfa—no corn, no hormones—and it roams freely, so the beef is low in fat, but tastes very rich." Let us not forget the grand fried plantains or the El Original—which originated during Pernot's stint at Rittenhouse Hotel—a Chilean sea bass set over sour-meets-sweet tamarind sauce. He used exotic ingredients from Cuba to Argentina and served them in seductive presentations unlike any other chef in the city.

Pernot's imaginative ceviches, nothing more than a curated list of high-quality fish cured in citrus and spices, were what kept the patrons coming back for more.

Brightly patterned fabrics, stripes and prints covered the banquettes and chairs. Pernot left nothing to chance, poking through thirty-five china outlets to find the right mix of Latin color and shapes. Servers dressed in Caribbean guayabera shirts bustled around the tropical Havana-inspired dining room, well trained to provide the right attention to detail toward all the dishes, some not even translated, on the menu. There was a tented courtyard dancing with palms, Latin music blasting, and a sultry flamenco dancer flashed on a mural behind the bar.

A tasting menu, served at the chef's bar, offered a good value and the best seat in the house—a long view into the chef's open kitchen.

John Mariani of *Esquire* named Pernot "Chef of the Year" in the December 1999 issue of the magazine, stating the chef was "perhaps the best exemplar of Nuevo Latino food in America." The year prior, Pernot was named one of *Food & Wine's* best cooks.

In May 2000, *Inquirer's* Craig Laban wrote that "Pernot's nightly ceviche set off Nuevo Latino sparks for the most exciting little dishes in town."

Pernot went on to publish a ceviche book in 2001, which features recipes like Bahian Lobster Ceviche with Passion Fruit Mojo and Grilled Papaya Salad, Spinach-Pine Nut Croquetas and Crispy Malanga Chips, plus sexy Latin cocktails such as Papi Sour and ¡Pasión!'s signature Caipirinha.

The Nuevo Latino trend was never hotter than when ¡Pasión! earned four bells in 2002. While owner of ¡Pasión!, Pernot earned an impressive list of accolades, including recognition from *Gourmet* magazine, *Philadelphia Magazine* and *Fodor's*.

In 2006, Chef Guillermo Pernot eventually left to oversee the kitchens at the Cuba Libre chain, where he remains chef and partner to this day. However, for many, they will never forget their first ¡Pasión! experience, where they enjoyed their first arepa tasting or delighted their taste buds with the chef's creative ceviche magic. Habanero with sturgeon? Lobster with passionfruit mojo? Sí!

¡Pasión! Recipe: Scallop Ceviche
Adapted from the Food Network
4 servings

1 pound fresh scallops
1 cup fresh lime juice
½ cup fresh orange juice
3 tablespoons diced red onion
2 tablespoons diced serrano peppers
3 tablespoons diced cachucha peppers

Place first 6 ingredients in a nonreactive container and keep cold in the refrigerator for 24 hours. Remove from refrigerator and drain all the liquid and set aside.

Sauce
2 tablespoons olive oil
½ pound tomatillos
½ pound Roma tomatoes
1 red onion
1 jalapeño pepper
½ cup lime juice
1 teaspoon truffle oil
1 bunch cilantro
Salt, pepper, to taste

In a sauté pan with tablespoon of oil, bring up to high heat and add first 4 sauce ingredients. Toss until they are blackened. Let cool, and in a food processor, place all blackened vegetables and remaining ingredients and pulse to medium chop the vegetables. Toss well and chill. Fold scallops into mixture and serve.

24

Knave of Hearts

230 South Street

Ty Bailey arrived in Philadelphia in 1973, penniless and shoeless. Raised in Connecticut, after a short, uncompleted stint at Tulane University studying art, Bailey found himself in Philadelphia after being nudged by a friend who was studying at the Pennsylvania Academy of Fine Arts. To get here, he hitchhiked. Along the way, he abandoned his moccasins because they hurt his feet.

He eventually rented a storefront for $175 a month with a girlfriend and a friend, a building that would become the core of his three-building restaurant, Knave of Hearts. He found work as a golf caddy and a dishwasher at the newly opened Astral Plane. At Astral, he worked his way up the line, from dishes to peeling potatoes, salads and eventually brunch cook.

Bailey's time at Astral Plane helped fuel his desire for a restaurant of his own. He saved up for a commercial range, then $350, and saved every penny to accumulate more restaurant equipment to outfit his rented storefront so it could accommodate twenty-two customers.

Inspired by a Maxfield Parrish children's book he picked up at a local flea market, *The Knave of Hearts*, he found a name for his restaurant, debuting the concept to the public in February 1975.

At first, his days were endless. He was the jack of all trades, from food buyer to prep cook and all-day cook. He had very little overhead.

Ty Bailey of the Knave of Hearts, once located at 230 South Street in Philadelphia, charmed date-night diners through the "restaurant renaissance" in the late '70s in his eclectic, mismatched dining room and bar. *Courtesy of Philadelphia Inquirer.*

The Knave became known for its fresh, upscale approach to the standard lunch menu and was a refreshing change of pace from the usual on South Street (no cheesesteaks here). Its laid-back, imaginative atmosphere made it one of the more relaxing dining rooms in the city, dressed with a mixture of hippie Victorian and postmodern kitsch. The drink selection was very good, especially the wonderful Bloody Mary, with a garnish that was a meal in itself.

The reinvention of the sandwiches made a substantial impact on South Philly diners. At any given time, you'd be able to find a fancifully dressed-up rendition of such things as challah layered with chicken, Roquefort dressing, arugula, basil and tropical fruit chutney or black bread smeared with an apple-spinach-macadamia-nut puree with marinated artichokes, pancetta and chevre.

Inquirer's Elaine Tait wrote in 1980 that the secret to Knave of Hearts' success went something like this:

> *Take one run-down, but upwardly mobile neighborhood, find an empty space...and make the interior spark with paint and imagination. Collect tables and chairs from second-hand furniture stories; collect china, flatware, glasses from flea markets and thrift shops. Avoid, at all costs, perfect matchups of patterns for table settings. Fill the store window with a jungle of greenery. Concoct a menu that mixes flavors as imaginatively as an artist mixes colors. Cook the dishes as though you were it for good friends. You've just found the formula for a successful storefront restaurant.*

Knave of Hearts' Recipe: Strawberry Soup

Strawberry soup was on the menu for Knave of Hearts' lifespan,
perfected with brandy, heavy cream and mint.
Adapted from the *Philadelphia Inquirer*, 1990
Makes 6 to 8 servings

2 quarts ripe strawberries
½ cup granulated sugar
½ cup water
1 (10-ounce) package frozen strawberries
¼ cup brandy
1 pint half-and-half, chilled
1 pint heavy cream, chilled
Mint, for garnish

Wash and hull fresh strawberries. In a 2½-quart saucepan, over medium heat, combine fresh strawberries, sugar and water. (The riper the strawberries, the sweeter the fruit. Less sweet fruit may require additional sugar.)

Bring mixture to a boil, and simmer for about 15 minutes or until berries are soft. Timing will vary dependent on the ripeness of the fruit. Stir in package of frozen berries until berries melt.

In a four-cup or larger saucepan, over medium heat, warm brandy. Then, working carefully away from overhead cabinets, flame the brandy and pour it over the strawberry base mixture and stir until well combined. The alcohol will continue to burn up to one minute. Remove from heat.

Strain the strawberry-brandy mixture to remove seeds and pulp. Soup may be made ahead to this point and chilled until serving time. When ready to serve, stir in half-and-half and heavy cream as desired. Serve chilled, garnished with fresh mint.

25

Astral Plane

The glasses were recycled sour cream jars. The silverware didn't match; neither did the china settings, the chairs or the table linens. Overhead, parachute-tented ceilings crowned crimson walls. Starlet photos and vintage robots lined the walls. A triumphant rattan chair adorned the dining room, reminiscent of Morticia Addams, and a phallic chandelier acted as the site's crown jewel. The floor was patched and unpolished. "Is this a serious restaurant or an exercise in shoestring decorating?" was one of the first published sentiments from *Philadelphia Inquirer*'s Elaine Tait.

It wasn't just the décor that made the space unique. The building's structural bones lent to a unique setup, with a greenhouse out back and a bar as you entered. The kitchen was gem box sized but large enough to execute a menu that made sense for the interesting space.

The cosmically funky atmosphere was what helped define and propel Astral Plane for its thirty-four-year run that began in 1973. It was so eclectic and, yes, *so '70s*. Words like *groovy*, *funky* and *hippie chic* were commonly thrown around when speaking about Astral Plane, and through the years it became a "time capsule of the city's first Restaurant Renaissance."

It was founded by brothers David and Robert Selke and their friend Reed Apaghian when they were young students in their early twenties. Originally, they intended to open an ice cream parlor and health food–focused place—even then that never went together.

"We opened with a vegetarian menu because we were all looking for new ways of eating," relayed Robert to the *Philadelphia Inquirer* during their opening year. "We were an immediate success, and that's lucky because we bought the food to open with our last money." (Robert opened Astral Plane with cooking experience under his belt, first getting his start at Déjà Vu.)

Eventually, Astral Plane evolved to a trendier restaurant, where one could enjoy large portions at reasonable prices and colorful presentations. Every course was served to you by a flighty server, wearing a funky T-shirt that fit the Astral Plane part.

Notable appetizers like shrimp wrapped in thin spring roll skins, deep-fried so crisp that they crackled with a touch of the tooth and served with a ginger sauce, kept guests coming back. Signature entrées included strawberry soup and the juicy and fruity chicken Tropicana—survivors for many years of the original menu—as well as honey sweetened chicken curry or Thai-style pork. Desserts were accorded a shrine-like display in the center of the dining room, branding themselves a triumphant spot at the end of all dinners.

Robert Strauss of the *Philadelphia Daily News* even reported in the early '80s that "Astral Plane had done a more than decent job in keeping up its cuisine." The menu was once described as somewhat of a melting pot, termed "Franco-Italian-Mexico-Asian." The menu also shifted through the years. When Kobe beef sliders and duck confit–stuffed egg rolls became a trend, you'd find them skirting out of the kitchen.

After all its years, this tiny spot never lost its charm. Its roster of celebrity customers was as diverse as its décor: through the years patrons included Divine, Donny Osmond, Sandra Day O'Connor, George Clooney, Whitney Houston, Bette Midler, Eric Lindros and Mick Jagger.

There was always an ample supply of drinks on hand to delight guests, and Sunday brunch featured the inexpensive "do-it-yourself" unlimited Bloody Mary bar, complete with premium vodka.

In July 2007, Astral Plane closed its doors as Philadelphia's Restaurant Renaissance was running a different course. Soon after, Versace glasses–wearing Catherine Fischer breathed fresh air into an Astral Plane 2.0. However, she removed the eclectic, quirky nature of the space that so many regulars loved, moving toward a stark white, elevated concept with higher price points and kitchen missteps. (It earned only one bell in Craig LaBan's review published during its debut year.)

Through the years to follow, several restaurants called 1708 Lombard Street home, including Keen and Midnight Iris.

26

Carman's Country Kitchen

1301 South Eleventh Street

The way Philly's funkiest and most eclectic bruncherie began was like how most things in owner-chef Carman Luntzel's life seem to have started—by asking herself, "Why not?" It all started in the late '80s when "a cousin to a friend of mine that I used to go with said this place was going to be changing hands, and he wanted me to take a ride with him to look at it," she revealed. "When I looked at the place, I said, 'What am I supposed to do with this, and he said, 'You'll think of something.'"

Luntzel came to Philly by way of Miami, opening nightclubs like she had done down south. Later, she transitioned her career to becoming a car salesman on Passyunk Avenue, first selling Pontiacs, then Dodges and Nissans. When the stock market took a hit, she needed something new. As a single mom of three, she needed something that worked within her schedule. So she took that tip from her friend of a friend and rented her restaurant from its then owner, Annie George, whose parents had run a restaurant there.

Luntzel hired a friend, Maggie Morningstar, to cook, and they went into business. After six months, Morningstar passed away suddenly. "I couldn't replace her," said Luntzel. "So that's what made Carman a cook. Nothing preplanned. None of this was."

Luntzel took ownership over her eight-by-ten-foot kitchen. She redid the menu to represent the food she grew up eating, plus offered up a plethora of specials that were inspired by her world travels. The "Country" in her restaurant's name wasn't referring to rural America but to the different countries of the world she visited.

She was never still. During a visit for breakfast, you'd catch the one-woman show slicing two-inch-thick slabs of challah, dunking them into a vat of French toast batter, then turning around to grab a few slices of bacon and talking to a guest—all from her tiny kitchen. She was graceful and efficient.

Carman Luntzel's unique eatery quickly became a neighborhood staple for more than twenty years. She changed the menu every week and never cooked from a recipe. It was rare that she repeated a dish.

The secret to her menu creativity was that, as she put it, she traveled a lot, had a phenomenal palate and possessed an imagination for what goes with what. "I [got] other people to eat food that I want to eat. It worked well for 22 years," she said. She was daring, too, even known to serve a side of *turtle*.

She stuck to a menu formula, which always included one pancake, one French toast, one omelet and one fish option, as well as suggested sides to go along with them. Diners would find options like impeccably cooked challah French toast with pineapple slices, Kentucky sour mash candied pecans, puréed pineapple, bananas, toasted coconut and crystallized ginger or French toast loaded with mangoes in a peach and pineapple sauce with Key lime graham cracker gelato crowning the top. Omelets would get folded with cheese, avocados, tomatoes, sweet onions, scallions and yucca with a hint of white anchovies and cilantro or salmon, corn, asparagus and ricotta salata. She even got customers to love sweetbreads and mushrooms, duck breast and sour cherries and conch fritters *for breakfast*.

The exception to the ever-changing menu was the catfish, which was always cracker-crusted catfish with her signature mix of crushed matzo, saltine, Ritz crackers, touch of graham crackers and cornflakes.

Carman possessed a special brand of hospitality with her boisterous personality. When regulars were asked why they kept coming back, they'd simply answer, "Carman." Luntzel paused to answer the phone. She did it all: taking orders, cooking the food and delivering it to tables. She refilled coffee and found time to chat with the customers she knew by first name.

Her space was small but mighty—like her. The seats were hard to come by, and sometimes food took an hour to leave the kitchen, but it was worth it. Three tables and a two-seat counter were up for grabs, and on warmer days, up to eight could score a seat around her famous outdoor table that was located in the bed of her pickup truck in front of the restaurant.

Her décor was the "Carman brand" in its own right—ding-a-ling-shaped ceramics peppered the shelves, as collected in her journeys around the world; phallus-adorned postcards clung to a corkboard; and a purplish rubber johnson dangled from the ceiling fan.

Carman's Country Kitchen was raved about in the *New York Times*. It scored promotion on TV and in magazines and was blogged about beyond belief. Luntzel's regulars come from South Philly, Center City and the 'burbs, as well as Alabama, Georgia, Texas, California, Minnesota, Japan and beyond.

"Carman's is absolutely unique and will be missed," said Therese Madden, a former producer for WHYY's *A Chef's Table*, adding, "Where else can you get a jelly bean omelet at Easter?"

In 1996, she closed for a month to escape to Spain to write a novella. She came back sans novel. The self-made chef eventually ended up closing the shop for good in December 2012 to move to South Carolina, but her contagious spirit and the one-of-a-kind Carman encounters regulars experienced over brunch live on.

Later, the established brunch spot's bricks became home to another breakfast destination: Comfort & Floyd.

27

Supper

926 South Street

At the height of the farm-to-table movement, chef Mitch Prensky introduced an urban farmhouse-style restaurant, Supper, on South Street in a former scooter shop. The restaurant was a follow-up to Global Dish, the catering business he and his wife, Jennifer Prensky, owned. It may have not been the first restaurant to serve dressed up deviled eggs—even if truffled—but it may have succeeded in being the first to serve the whole pig. He soaked smoked wings in birch beer and served them with buttermilk dressing and made them *fancy*.

Supper was celebrated for its rustic approach to fine dining. For a two-story farmhouse-inspired restaurant, it was well dressed with its cool hammered-copper exterior, exposed-beam ceilings and artsy light sculptures. It had the air of California sophistication floating through its walls.

Prensky's menus were a celebration of the farms from which he sourced the ingredients. (This was well before one of his partners started the seventy-five-acre Blue Elephant Farm in Newtown Square in 2009 and thus grew exclusively for the restaurant.) Since the ingredients were harvested locally, this meant the menus changed per the season; winter meant root vegetables and apples, while summer was more generous to the warm-weathered produce. What the chef would pick in the morning would end up on the menu that night. There was even a daily harvest menu, available at twenty-nine dollars for three courses, that celebrated the produce collected from the farm that day.

Chef Mitch Prensky's urban farmhouse-style restaurant, Supper, defined the way the city thought about farm-to-table dining, known for pastrami-fried chicken and fluffy baked biscuits. *Courtesy of* Philadelphia Magazine.

But Supper was a meat lover's delight too, serving charcuterie boards consisting of boudin blanc, country pâté and pork rillettes. Lunch featured house-made hot dogs made entirely of pork shoulder. Duck confit with pecan-sage waffles was a favorite, as was the ten-ounce LaFrieda blend burger.

Superb decadence lay in the dessert course with sugary delights like the Butterfinger torte with salted peanut ice cream or the sweet potato bundt cake with bourbon syrup and toasted marshmallow ice cream. We can't forget about brunch and the epic red velvet waffles that took Philadelphia by storm, as did the Bloody Marys that were built with a backbone of homemade pickles.

Every Tuesday brought a twenty-five-dollar fried chicken dinner special, featuring pastrami-fried chicken halves with Thousand Island dressing, house pickles, a biscuit and a side. The biscuits themselves stole the show, which is why Prensky expanded into his Scratch Biscuits offshoot on Chestnut Street in the spring of 2015.

After the opening of Scratch Biscuits, in October, Supper shuttered its doors after eight and a half years of service. The husband-and-wife duo attributed the closure to allowing them to focus on growing their other business, including their catering company. Eventually, Prensky went on to become the director of culinary for Hyatt Hotels.

Through Supper's acclaimed run, where the owners executed a flawless urban farmhouse concept from start to finish, they received distinct, well-earned honors: being recognized by a three-bell review by *Philadelphia Inquirer*, as well as a three-time placement in the top-50 restaurants of Philadelphia and a four-time Best of Philadelphia restaurant by *Philadelphia Magazine*. On a national level, they received recognition from the *New York Times*, James Beard Foundation, Food Network, *Gourmet*, *Bon Appétit*, *Food & Wine* and *Plate Magazine*.

Supper Recipe: Virginia Peanut Soup, Smoked Bacon, Pickled Peach, Green Onion
Serves 4

1 large piece bacon, diced
2 tablespoons butter
1 ½ cups diced onion
1 garlic clove, minced
2 teaspoons fresh chopped ginger
2 tablespoons flour
¼ cup bourbon
6 cups chicken stock
1 ½ cups dry-roasted peanuts

1 teaspoon Worcestershire sauce
2 teaspoons hot sauce
½ teaspoon salt
¼ teaspoon freshly ground black pepper
4 ounces smoked bacon lardons
4 ounces pickled peaches, diced
2 ounces green onion, julienned

Render bacon in butter. Add onion, garlic and ginger and sweat. Add flour and cook flour out until not raw (as if making a roux). Add bourbon and reduce. Add chicken stock and peanuts and cook for 30 to 45 minutes. Finish with Worcestershire and hot sauce and purée in a high-speed blender. Pass through a chinois and season to taste. Garnish each bowl with bacon lardons, pickled peaches and green onion.

28

Zanzibar Blue

Originally 305 South Eleventh Street; Relocated to 600 North Broad Street

After a trip in the mid-'80s to Togo, Africa, Robert Bynum, then thirty-four, was inspired to bring the lively nightlife scene to the States. With a goal to do his part to reshape Philadelphia's nightlife and breathe life into it, he partnered with his brother Benjamin, then twenty-eight, to open Zanzibar Blue in 1990 in Washington Square West, at Eleventh Street between Spruce and Pine. The intent was to open a cosmopolitan restaurant meets jazz café.

Music was in the brothers' blood, after all. Their father, Ben Bynum Sr., ran one of Philly's funkiest discotheques, Club Impulse, throughout the '70s and before that the Cadillac Club at 3738 Germantown Avenue. Robert was a Wharton School grad, Benjamin a restaurant industry vet, having worked at such places as Apropos and Zocalo, and Benjamin agreed to attend the Restaurant School once he and his brother planned to open Zanzibar Blue.

The brothers even confessed that their family was always intrinsically connected to their entertainment business, with entertainers like Aretha Franklin visiting their family home when she was in town to perform.

The restaurant's name was even music influenced, inspired by "Blue Gardenia" by Dinah Washington, one of Robert's favorite songs. "In fact, that was going to be the name, but it was already registered," he said. "Zanzibar" was also cited to nod to their African connection, where the whole idea sparked from.

Zanzibar Blue was a premier jazz nightclub—and it was spacious, yet intimate. It took a staff of twenty-seven to run the dining room that sat sixty-eight, a lounge that sat up to forty and a jazz café that held fifty-five. It was the first of its kind for Philadelphia, and it went beyond its nightly live music to the kitchen, which came with high-caliber culinary standards, receiving high marks across the board for its food, service and wine.

To match the creativity of the established music scene, there were creative riffs coming from the kitchen as well. The global menu ran the gamut from grilled Atlantic salmon wrapped in Parma ham, rock shrimp tempura and Amaretto cream-topped and shrimp-filled ravioli, to down-home fried catfish with red beans, rice and collard greens. The Provençale seafood soup met fanfare, served in a big bowl full of shrimp, scallops, clams and veggies in a saffron-scented fish stock. You could never miss the sweet potato cheesecake for dessert, either.

By 1994, the Bynum brothers had become synonymous with the local jazz scene, with reporters suggesting that "first came Zanzibar Blue, second came the local jazz scene." It wasn't long before the biggest names in the jazz industry started showing up to perform at Zanzibar. The brothers also increased their involvement beyond their jazz club in Philadelphia's music scene, branching out to co-produce concerts at the Painted Bride Art Center or the Barclay Hotel.

Seizing on the impending development of the Avenue of the Arts, in 1996 the club moved to the Bellevue on the Avenue in a much larger space. It replaced a watering hole named Mick's, offering Zanzibar Blue guests a more supper club–style layout with 150 seats to dine and 60 at the bar. Here was where they hosted jazz and blues greats; being a larger venue, they could afford bigger names, including Nancy Wilson, Lou Rawls, Grover Washington Jr., Jimmy Scott, Steve Tyrell, Chick Corea, Arturo Sandoval and Chuck Mangione.

The atmosphere was rich and clubby, done in shades of black and red, with tiny lamps glowing on mirrored walls amid vintage photos of jazz greats. Of course, the brothers integrated a high-tech sound system in the space—which cost more than $15,000—that cranked Billie Holiday and Ella Fitzgerald when live acts were on break. For its time, it was sexy and cool. There was a long, graceful bar that was always well stocked; you could always count on a good glass of wine and an exotic beer or liquor. You didn't have to dress up to come there, though many people did, which lent to the overall elegance of the place.

"The music and the people-watching [were] so much fun," scribed Jim Quinn for the *Philadelphia Inquirer* in 1990.

"This is one of those rare bars where you feel as if you're really going out—every night is an event," wrote Jim and Lisa Anderson in *Philly's Best Bars of 1992.*

It was always recommended that you come early, as seats were always at a premium. If there was not a live jazz performance going on, then there was a party or a political fundraiser. There were often jazz happy hours during the week, and smooth-jazz station WJJZ-FM broadcasted Sunday jazz brunches from the club.

In 2002, the cheekily nicknamed "Blues Brothers" introduced a new Zanzibar Blue location in Wilmington, Delaware, on the ground floor of the Brandywine Building in a former bank. After the brothers explored New York, D.C. and Baltimore, Wilmington's mayor convinced them to open downtown in support of his effort to get people to stay and live there. When the location opened, Al Paris of Chestnut Hill's Paris Bistro acted as executive chef.

Quoted as "arguably the city's best-known jazz venue," Zanzibar Blue announced it would close on April 29, 2007, after more than ten years downstairs at the Bellevue at Broad. Robert Bynum told the *Inquirer* that the lease was up and that although he was satisfied with the building and location, "we didn't think it was in our best interests to renew. We'd rather own [our] building than lease.'" (The new lease was said to have nearly doubled the rent.)

Zanzibar Blue's closing was a blow to Philadelphia's jazz scene, once a hotbed of national acts and audiences who packed such joints as the Blue Note, Pep's and the Showboat.

Years after the closure, Jenice Armstrong of the *Philadelphia Daily News* published an article relishing in what the Blues Brothers built. As she wrote: "[Zanzibar Blue's] unexpected closing two years ago caught jazz lovers by surprise and left a gaping hole in the local scene—not to mention my own social life. I haven't been out to listen to jazz since the restaurant shuttered. Not even once."

She went on to suggest that Zanzibar Blue was "as much a part of the city's social fabric as Old Original Bookbinders, Penn's Landing, and Pat's Steaks. It was where you took out-of-towners you wanted to impress. It was Philadelphia's answer to Harlem, New York's legendary Sylvia's Restaurants or D.C.'s Blues Alley."

Years after Zanzibar's twelve-year legacy came to an end, the Bynum brothers debuted South in the same Broad Street space, a southern-inspired reincarnation that continued to provide a space for high-profile jazz performers.

The Bynum brothers continued to be serial restaurateurs, opening Warmdaddy's, a blues club first in Old City and now in South Philadelphia; Relish, a jazz theme in West Oak Lane that's become Philly's power lunch spot; Heirloom, a now-closed BYOB in partnership with chef Al Paris; Paris Bistro, again with Al Paris—in which they recently sold their share; and Green Soul, a health-forward fast-casual restaurant with southern influences.

29

Black Banana

Third and Race Streets

T he man whom many restaurant critics credit with the Philadelphia restaurant revival is Xavier Hussenet. First, he was accredited for his pioneering spirit, repetitively going where no other restaurant had gone before. In 1972, he opened in what was said to be no-man's land, Fourth and South Streets—first an ice cream parlor, the La Banane Noire. He took what was said to be a decaying area of the city and brought it to life. The concept quickly transitioned from ice cream to French food, but the original name—one of the place's ice cream concoctions—stuck, albeit shifted to its Americanized version, Black Banana. The restaurant's success helped change the neighborhood, with more than a half-dozen other restaurants coming to the area to open.

Then came another "wasteland," around Third and Race Streets, where he looked to repeat the same success as South Street. This time he had a liquor license, and the move occurred in 1976, attributed to the escalating rent at the original location, plus the need for more space.

In an effort to provide entertainment beyond dining, Café Za Za was introduced in early 1978 in the upstairs room of the Black Banana restaurant. Intended to provide late-night snacks for the after-theater crowd, the late-night menu was served Mondays through Saturdays until 1:00 a.m. featuring such specialties as quiche, cheese platters and two crepes, one specifically named the lengthy "Jack Jones' All-Time Favorite Chicken Crepe." The upstairs' club also featured a signature drink, the "Kiss," which was a $2.50 mix of Kriter champagne, a splash of crème de cassis and a touch of Armagnac.

In 1978, *Philadelphia Inquirer*'s Elaine Tait reported that Xavier Hussenet had been offering nouvelle cuisine for three years, featuring daily specials—from softshell crabs and red snapper to fresh morels, zucchini and figs—inspired by his trips to local markets.

In 1979, Hussenet returned from a trip to his homeland (France) and was the first chef to introduce gourmand cooking in Philadelphia through a pocketful of recipes and ideas. At the time, the French trend of *cuisine gourmande* was sweeping their country; chefs were starting to say "to hell with it, let's eat," as a backlash against low-calorie cookery that trended in the 1970s. He actually brought menus back from all the restaurants and meals he enjoyed while abroad, as evidence that things like pink peppercorns and cilantro as well as raspberry vinegar and duck were all the rage. (Some of Philadelphia's food critics asked to dig into the menus as evidence.)

In 1980, Hussenet was having Parisian fresh foie gras flown in from Paris, selling a one-and-a-half-ounce serving for eighteen dollars apiece.

Eventually, in true Black Banana fashion, the restaurant went through more changes in 1981, including introducing a private club, the Crusaders Community Club, which gave the restaurant the option of late-night hours and required a guest register and membership. The club became Black Banana's focus from the '80s to the early '90s. The guest register required members to share things like their age, vocation, height, weight and sexual orientation, which would enable Black Banana to send invites to exclusive parties based on members' interests. Quickly, the upstairs club became popularized for its wacky costume parties, including a swimsuit beauty contest where the contestants were men and women were the judges.

The club continued to thrive through the '80s for its appreciation of cutting-edge fashion and music. This period of time was marked by such legendary talents as Josh Wink, Robbie Tronco, King Britt, Dozia, Toni Thomas and Philly it girl Kim Kelly.

The Black Banana suffered a devastating fire in 1991, with the staff working night and day to rebuild the club, while loyal patrons held vigils out on its sidewalks. The club's co-founder and partner of Hussenet, Garrick Melmeck, succumbed to AIDS in the months following the fire.

Kirk Beckman ultimately assumed ownership and management of the club until its demise in 1998. The building now houses Wexler Fine Arts Gallery.

In 2011, a former DJ and promoter of the Black Banana, Nick London, hosted a reunion at Voyeur. "They essentially created a European nightlife experience in Philly," he relayed to *Philadelphia Magazine*. "And they did things that no other club was doing at the time. Sometimes they would even change the entrance to the club."

"Plenty of celebrities also came to the club over the years," he continued.

> *But the one story I love the most is the night Prince came to the Black Banana. His people called ahead and had an area of the club roped off for when he arrived. I was the DJ that night and was running a video of all-black jive dancing from the '20s. His security man came over to the DJ booth and asked if I would play the video again. Minutes later the guy came back with a signed album that said, "Love God, Prince." I was thrilled!*

30

Tashan

777 South Broad Street

Munish Narula already knew what most Philadelphians thought about Indian restaurants before he opened the ultra-luxe Tashan. He knew most thought Indian food was cheap, super-spicy takeout or meant a $9.99 buffet, where tables were crammed and the walls were a dull shade of yellow. He wanted to present Indian food in a new, elevated manner.

Narula was no stranger to Indian food, and he earned the right to be critical. He first began redefining Indian food when he launched Tiffin, his Philadelphia-based delivery and takeout empire in 2006. He started with humble beginnings in a small Northern Liberties space and quickly expanded into a multi-restaurant empire with more than two hundred seats, a delivery team and a reputation for serving the better takeout Indian food.

But he wanted more. It was what *Inquirer*'s Craig LaBan billed as Tiffin's "big Buddakan moment." It was set to be a game-changer, to show how Indian food could be done upscale if you have the best ingredients and sophisticated chefs at the helm. (It wasn't the first time the city experienced a similar elevated Indian concept—Valerie Safran and Marcie Turney tried their hand at it with Bindi, which closed in 2011, the same year Tashan opened.)

With Tashan, Narula's goal was to take Indian food to a new level and make it more approachable. "We throw the word 'sexy' around as a joke. But we do want to make it sexy," he said. (The name Tashan was derived from Hindi, meaning "style, swagger or attitude.")

Munish Narula's Tashan was Philadelphia's most luxe Indian restaurant, inspired by elevating Indian food in a new manner that the city hadn't seen before. *Courtesy of Philadelphia Magazine.*

An interesting element of the concept was that the chef was the Haitian-born Sylva Senat, who worked at Jean-Georges and Aquavit in New York before moving on to Buddakan in New York and then Philly. "We started to ask, 'Why do we need an Indian chef?'" Narula said. "We needed someone who would look at the food from a totally different perspective."

It was ambitious, high-end and a well-executed new-modern Indian spot. Vast in 136 seats and designed by New York–based designer Winka Dubbledam, it managed to be sultry while still being intimate. There was a private wine room separated by pivoting leather doors, oversized chairs in the lounge and a deep alcove of banquettes lending the feel of semi-privacy. Tashan had wine lists on iPads—something well before its time then, and it experienced celebrity sightings, from Hollywood mainstays Harrison Ford and Gary Oldman to Bollywood film legends like Anupam Kher.

In all its glory, the food was the most interesting element of the grandeur of Tashan. The kitchen took creative liberties but still stayed true to tradition on traditional dishes. Highlights included a spinach patty stuffed with a paneer-pistachio center and finished with a French saffron and morel mushroom cream sauce. The kitchen wood-smoked Vermont quail Rajasthan style and served it in a waft of aromatic smoke. The crispy *golgappa* was topped with mint-cilantro water; lamb chops were tenderized by papaya marinade and a touch of pure mustard oil. And more classic dishes, which were few and far between, were so elegant that even the *Inquirer*'s Craig LaBan said it was "the best he ever had." (Oh, and there was no samosa to be found unless you came for brunch.)

After a four-year stint, Tashan closed its doors in September 2015, attributing its demise to the fact that it never became the hard-to-get-reservation spot that it hoped for. It didn't help that the opening chef, James Beard–nominated Senat, departed in the summer of 2013, losing some flair without his handiwork in the kitchen. Since the owner also backed Tiffin, it was a challenge for locals to understand it wasn't Tiffin but something so much more.

Toward the end of Tashan's time, *Philadelphia Magazine* writer Jason Sheehan wrote that he blamed Tashan struggles on Philadelphians:

> *Right now, Tashan is one of the best Indian restaurants in the country—up there with places like Rasika in Washington, D.C.—but you're not going. Why? Because you have it in your mind that Indian food ought to be confined to buffets and menus that top out at $10? Because you have to go a couple blocks out of your way to find it? That's ridiculous.*

31

Holly Moore's Upstairs Cafe

123 South Eighteenth Street

Before Hollister "Holly" Moore was one of Philadelphia's pioneering food bloggers and after he helped the McDonald's Corporation launch the Big Mac, he opened his namesake restaurant, Holly Moore's Upstairs Cafe, near Rittenhouse Square after graduating from the Restaurant School of Philadelphia. Holly Moore's was a culmination of what Holly loved the most: approachable, affordable neighborhood fare created with respect (i.e., pasta made from scratch).

Located in a district that notably held high-end, high-rent restaurants from 1978 to 1982, Moore's literally upstairs second-floor café (with its kitchen on the third floor) was poised on the northeast corner of Eighteenth and Sansom Streets, then across from Neil Stein's Fish Market and within a half-block walk from Steven Poses's Frog Commissary.

Many would climb the twenty-one uncomfortably steep stairs to escape from the hustle and bustle of Center City nightlife. Upon reaching the top, guests were delightfully presented with a cosmopolitan loft with tables on two levels and long, un-curtained windows with a striped awning outside for shade.

Dick Cheverton of the *Philadelphia Daily News* wrote in 1979 that the restaurant was part of the city's "boom in chic, 'bare-wood' restaurants," one lined with "bare Formica-topped tables, paper napkins, industrial lighting fixtures"—all of which was nice, but not overdone.

Elaine Tait of the *Philadelphia Inquirer* wrote the same year that the restaurant itself was a "series of surprises starting with its name. The name itself caused so much confusion that Holly joked earlier on that he would have buttons made for the women on his staff saying, 'I'm not Holly.'"

"The menu [was] also a surprise," she wrote. "Imaginative cold entrees such as *vitello tonnato*, salads, and sandwiches." The menu was prepared out of a tiny, visible kitchen, which busted out inventive, nifty eating for lunch, dinner and snacking.

The food was said to be "sandwich shop-chic." Ubiquitous crocks of "world famous" chili con queso, a cheap red wine–splashed adaptation of a recipe that became famous in Hollywood courtesy of Chasen's, would be the leading order. Others would stay loyal to the select, more elevated dishes like the chicken liver and apple mousse spiked with Armagnac or the daily special of curry with chutney and sambal. Tait reported that the quiche Lorraine was a "felicitous version of the classic that housed a light, delicious filling in a well-made pastry crust." There were also health-focused salads and sandwiches, a testament to the calorie-crunchers of its time.

Desserts were on display as you'd arrive, with a variety of classic cakes. Moore respected Nadine Gearhart's craft as a baker; she busied herself with from-scratch versions of Sachertorte, German chocolate cake and memorable lemon cake adorned with marzipan ducks. There was no shortage of espresso and lattes prepped from one heavy-duty machine, then said to be "exotic," "European" and quite a progressive way to end a meal well before the coffee craze took America.

Moore's café did offer breakfast hours a few years in, calling the menu "civilized, a way to wake up gently." Eggs benedict with country pâté and mustard hollandaise, melon wrapped in prosciutto and fresh baked croissants were often on the menu.

In April 1980, Moore snagged a liquor license and introduced a drink program with an extensive wine list. In summer 1981, Moore introduced a second food operation, an outdoor pop-up at the Philadelphia Zoo, offering interesting alternates to the usual hot dog and burger fare. By 1982, Moore's café was under new ownership and eventually closed.

In 2000, Holly Moore began his ever-popular, straight-shooting HollyEats.com review site, popularizing a rating system built around grease stains (the more stains, the better the restaurant) and a celebrated "Hot Dog Page" with nearly 160 reviews of hot dog joints. A lifelong friend of Moore's wrote after Moore's passing in 2017, "I don't know anybody who loved food as much as him, or who loved Philadelphia as much as he did."

During his years in Philadelphia, he also opened a self-service copy shop, operated a military-style exercise program at the Ritz and was a food columnist for the *Philadelphia City Paper*. Moore even received the honor of a caricature displayed on the walls of the Palm restaurant and became known as the city's "anti-foodie."

PART VII

UNFORGETTABLE
COMFORT FOOD CLASSICS

32
Little Pete's

219 South Seventeenth Street

Center City Philadelphia still mourns the passing of the cash-only twenty-four-hour diner Little Pete's, which graced the corner of Seventeenth and Chancellor Streets for nearly forty years. Until May 2017, no late night in Rittenhouse Square was complete without a trip to this iconic spot for something from the well-worn griddle.

Little Pete's was named after Pete Koutroubas, a Greek immigrant who started in the restaurant industry as a dishwasher and busboy. He was so short that in order to do his job, he needed to stand on a milk crate. That's where the nickname came from.

"Because I used to work at Eagle II diner, and the owner was 'Big Pete'—he was six-foot something," Pete said in 2015 to *Philadelphia Magazine*. "And there was a manager there who was 'Pete.' And I was the busboy—I was the little one at 5-foot-3. They used to call them Big Pete, Middle Pete and Little Pete."

Pete came from Greece to Philadelphia in June 16, 1972, when he was fourteen. Six years later, in 1978, he opened Little Pete's. "I was young," he said. "I wanted to open my own place. I knew how to cook a little bit. Plus, my mother was helping out, and she was a really good cook. I just turned 20 when I opened the business."

(Before Little Pete's was a twenty-four-hour diner, the location was one of the eighteen Philly-based Dewey's coffee shops. Its claim to fame was in May 1965, when it hosted the first successful sit-in for LGBT+ rights.)

His "Little Pete" name, in red script on a white, old-fashioned sign, became an iconic signal to a place that invited people to cozy into simple booths or onto a stool stationed around a U-shaped counter.

Little Pete's 1,500-square-foot size helped contribute to its longevity. "You know why it was one of the best?," he continued. "Because it was small. Two waitresses, two dishwashers, two cooks, one cashier. When you have a big restaurant, you need extra help. And still you're only busy a couple of hours a day, for lunch and dinner. We were always busy."

You could always find Pete behind the grill. He was committed day in and out to the diner's success. "Every day, I come here three in the morning," he relayed. "I [did] all my dressings, all my sauces, everything. I leave here from one or two o'clock. I go home for an hour, then I come back for dinnertime, and leave at nine o'clock. Seven days a week."

When asked what it is like running a twenty-four-hour diner, Pete confessed: "The first two years, there was no day off. It was six in the morning to 12 at night."

People came and continued to come for four decades, sucking down chocolate milkshakes and slices of strawberry shortcake, Reubens, double-decker turkey clubs and endless orders of French fries and mozzarella sticks.

It was like *Cheers*—but without alcohol. Part of the charm was the waitstaff, who, if you came once, would remember your order. Debbie Pegolese, sixty-three, of South Philadelphia, worked as a waitress at Little Pete's on and off for a dozen years.

"There are a lot of regulars who come in here because this is their time to talk to somebody," she shared with the *Philadelphia Inquirer* in 2017. "They don't have anybody at home. Some don't even have kitchens. Once I was out with my kids, and I said, 'There goes iced-tea-chicken-cheesesteak.'"

Waitress Margie Storn was a Little Pete's mainstay, working shifts for thirty years, typically manning the late-night crowd. She told WHYY that scene was always the "most entertaining."

"They were hungry enough that they go up to a complete stranger and take a French fry off their plate. Sometimes it's funny, and sometimes they're throwing French fries around," she said. The interactions that unfold when two people from totally different backgrounds sit cheek-to-jowl have always been memorable, she said.

Similar to Pegolese, she had a customer that she called "neither/either because he doesn't want a pickle or a chip, so that's how we remember him."

In early October 2015, the Philadelphia City Council voted in favor of a critical zoning change to the site of Little Pete's, which would allow

New York developers to build a luxury hotel where the diner resided. By January 2016, speculation of what would happen to Little Pete's resulted in a trending #SAVELITTLEPETES campaign that expanded onto social media. Locals were not going to give up without a fight for their favorite neighborhood diner.

Rent had continued to skyrocket since Little Pete's got its start. In the '70s, Pete's monthly rent was $800. In 2017, it was $10,000.

On Memorial Day 2017, Pete announced he would be closing with a block party that would take over Chancellor Street on the Tuesday after. The party was a success, with a few thousand guests, wine and a band playing Greek music. "I've been here thirty-nine years. I know a lot of people," he laughed at the time.

After the closing announcement, celebrities and locals alike came out of the woodwork to share their stories. Comedian John Hodgman posted a goodbye tribute on Instagram. (Prior to that, in 2015, he published a Tumblr rant, in which he said the diner was his "favorite scrapple counter in the world," and pleaded for folks to help protect the diner from being destroyed by the impending hotel project.) Another popular comedian, Paul F. Tompkins, joined Hodgman in sharing his fond farewell to the beloved diner.

A photography book, *Final Days of Little Pete's* by Michael Penn, was even released to honor the closing and pay tribute to the point in time.

For a while, professional boxer Joe Frazier would come by every day. Rick "Chainsaw" LaPointe, a longtime guitar technician for Bruce Springsteen and Billy Joel, told *Billy Penn* that he and his bandmates "always tended to hit Little Pete's. I always seem to find myself there for something."

The Facebook page for Little Pete's remains live today. Repeat guests have left their love letters to the diner. John Petsinger shared a tale: "One morning, I stopped for breakfast and was embarrassed not to have enough to pay the bill. The waitress told me she knew my face, not to worry, but come back later to pay. Later I came back with money and flowers. I'll miss their personal touch."

When *Philadelphia Magazine* asked Little Pete how he felt about the outpouring of support he received after announcing he was closing, he said, "Everybody loves us. We've been there 37 years. People grew up there [and eventually] brought their kids there."

Billy Penn did a call for Little Pete's stories in March 2017, just before it was set to close its doors. One couple shared that toward the beginning of their courtship, Little Pete's was a meeting point between their locations (one living in Collingswood, New Jersey, another in Ambler, Pennsylvania). It was their "end-of-the-date-but-not-wanting-it-to-ever-end-spot" that was nurtured over slices of pie in a two-seat booth.

Others discussed the hospitality of the waitstaff, confessing it was there, in Little Pete's over their regular order of chocolate cake with a side of fries that they were able to feel like Philly was home. Another retold his story to the *Philadelphia Inquirer* of doing a face plant into his stuffed cabbage and being taken care of by the owner himself until the ambulance arrived. Every visit of his after was welcomed with a "how's your health?"

Another fan, Joe Tolstoy, shared with WHYY that he used to work a late-night shift at the Bellevue-Stratford Hotel. When he was finished, he'd swing by Little Pete's for both the mozzarella sticks and the humanity.

Interestingly enough, in the wake of Little Pete's demise, Cherry Hill native Matthew Cahn, who grew up eating the Texas Tommy, a split griddled hot dog with bacon and cheese, was inspired to open Middle Child to celebrate and continue Philadelphia's appreciation for well-crafted sandwiches.

"I had moved away from Philly, and every time I came home another classic spot had closed," he explained to the *Courier Post* in January 2018. "It started with Snow White, then Salumeria, then Little Pete's and Sarcone's. Philly is the land of the sandwich, but when these places closed it felt like a real loss." Cahn's sandwich spot continues to fill the void left behind from lunch legends, scoring national press from such publications as *Bon Appétit*.

Ioannis "John" Koutroubas, Pete's brother, said the silver lining of Pete's closing was he could have a break. At the time of the closing, he "hadn't had a vacation in eleven years."

In 1993, they opened a second Little Pete's in Fairmount, located in the Philadelphian. It remains open to this day.

33

Shank's & Evelyn's

932 South Tenth Street

Shank's & Evelyn's quintessential luncheonette opened in the Italian Market back in 1962, on Tenth Street near Montrose, back when Johnny Carson launched late-night TV and the Beatles had invaded America. Founded by husband-and-wife team Frank "Shank" Perri and Evelyn, the popular midday spot was a true South Philly experience, with "slam-it-down" wait service and "what kinda samwidge ya want?" spewing from the all-female, all-related counter-service staff.

Prior to opening the lunch spot, Perri started worked at a battery and tire garage. There, he started making hot dogs and other food and giving it away to customers. "That gave him the idea to start the restaurant," relayed his son, Frank Jr. History also revealed that a grandfather had a tire shop in the location that Shank and his wife took over for their counter.

It was an original hole-in-the-wall luncheonette. It was petite, checkered with black-and-white tiles and lined with six tables and six barstools. There was no menu, just a board that listed the mainstay items and prices and a few hand-lettered specials perched up on cardboard taped over the grill.

With an iconic RC awning crowning its exterior, it served folks from all walks of life, from politicians and actors to lawyers, doctors, sports personalities and the locals from the neighborhood. Together, they all shared a love of old-fashioned Sicilian cuisine served with only fresh ingredients, in large portions and at modest prices. Plus, repeat patrons particularly liked their breakfast and lunch served with the side of sass you always got at Shank's & Evelyn's.

The family served authentic, really home-style Italian food that became a true Philadelphia original, from long strips of crisp-fried eggplant and red sauces to a beautifully crunchy chicken cutlet, thinly breaded and pan-fried—and "never deep-fried!" The roast pork sandwiches dripped with freshly sautéed spinach, originally priced at seventy-nine cents.

If you'd opt for the roast beef combo instead, a big bowl of gravy would make your acquaintance, meant to be spooned onto the roast beef, as would a side of pickled tomatoes.

The Giambotti, an infamous omelet built with everything but the kitchen sink, came in one size—serving two. You couldn't order it after noon. It was an outrageous omelet that was almost impossible to finish, but a must-have Philly breakfast experience. It started out on the flat top with peppers and onions, sausage and "this, that, the other," and then at the end, five eggs were cracked over the ingredients.

Locals would love to visit to listen to the colorful conversations that could only be heard in a neighborhood that takes pride in its old-world charm.

For forty-eight years, the all-woman counter staff would tell you, following Evelyn's lead, that in "South Philly, the way to a person's heart is through their stomach."

The operation was always a family affair. Evelyn, her sister, daughters, cousins—they were all behind the counter. You may have had to wait for a table, but it was worth it.

In 1994, Frank "Shank" passed from emphysema, with Evelyn and family continuing to carry on the family's legacy.

In its later years, you'd see Evelyn's daughter Pamela Poppa spending the morning in the kitchen with her tongs, frying her signature eggplant in the roasting pan set over four burners of the commercial stove. Next were the veal cutlets, then the heap of chicken cutlets that were, indeed, "classic Italian." (Twenty-five to thirty pounds were made on a good day.)

What was so special about their iconic chicken cutlets? "There's no secret to them," she shared with the *Inquirer* in the late '90s. "They're simple. I enjoy them and we've got lots of customers that love 'em too."

In true Philly fashion, the chicken cutlet sandwiches were served with garlicky greens, hot peppers and sharp provolone.

At the same time, Evelyn's other daughter, Donna Mahan, and a cousin by marriage, Theresa Belardo, would knock out potato-and-egg sandwiches and pancakes on the flat top. Soon, they'd be prepped for the day's lunch service, with succulent pork roasts ready for the slicer, steaming escarole soup and platters of various cutlets, waiting to be devoured by the guests that would take up residence on the site's nine counter stools and five tables. Evelyn's sister, Marian Costa, would eventually join the crew to help serve customers.

In 2007, dinners were launched at the institution, a follow-up to the short-lived Frankie's at Night project led by Shank and Evelyn's son, Frankie Perri. In 1997, he reinvented the room above Shank's & Evelyn's with a tablecloth restaurant seating thirty-eight guests. A rotating crew of relatives and neighborhood friends poured complimentary pitchers of homemade wine. For such a small space, his eighteen dollars or less dinner plates packed big flavor, featuring his self-taught versions of Calabrian cooking—all smothered in red sauces and rich stocks, sparked with good vinegar and fresh herbs and made with quality ingredients.

Perri, in speaking about his cooking at Frankie's, would articulate that he'd "whack it up, and give it a little zippity-doo-da!" And that he did, through seafood pasta medleys like shrimp scampi and spicy tomato cioppino or lobster *fra diavolo* and creamy veal medallions.

There into the nighttime hours you could enjoy stuffed clams and Italian antipasti consisting of romaine dressed with artichokes, mozzarella, sun-dried tomatoes, prosciutto, salami, olives and roasted peppers. Pan-fried ziti and heartier meat options like the "Steak Frankie's Way," a filet mignon topped with roasted peppers, onions, mushrooms and tomatoes in a demi-glace cognac sauce, were also on the menu. Every dish came with a side of pasta in red sauce, which wasn't really needed due to the obscene-sized portions of entrées like chicken Francese. For dessert, there were strawberries soaked in Grand Marnier with house-made whipped cream, and at first bite, it was as though you were taking a shot.

In 2008, Shank's & Evelyn's chicken cutlet sandwich nabbed a spot in *Esquire*'s "Encyclopedia of Sandwiches" issue.

Once the rumor mill spread about the original Shank's moving, in 2009, folks came out of the woodwork: "One was from a shop owner in the Italian Market, a block away, who'd brought in chefs Jacques Pepin and Pierre Franey, quietly soliciting Evelyn to pay special attention to their plates. 'I don't care who they are,' Evelyn boomed to the *Philadelphia Inquirer*. 'Everybody here gets treated the same!'"

Local novelist Ken Kalfus remembered taking in unshaven *Chicago Hope* star Peter Berg and his table getting a notably solicitous, over-the-top, flirtatious welcome.

Robert Picardo, East Falls native, always ate at Shank's & Evelyn's when he starred in local musicals, such as *Gemini: The Musical*. His best friend, Joe Pantoliano, was a repeat guest while in town filming *The In Crowd* in the mid-'80s.

"It's like eating in my mother's kitchen; the food [was] phenomenal," shared Bob Santoro, a frequent patron of Shank's & Evelyn's. "The sauces, the greens, the peppers—it is like what you would get at home."

When Philadelphia councilman Joe Vignola was just a practicing lawyer, he remembered going to Shank's as a place that was like "going home. Once you [took] a bite of their sandwich, you know why you have to wait so long to get another one," he recalled.

Congressman Tom Foglietta called Shank's & Evelyn's "a great part of Philadelphia—and especially South Philadelphia. The luncheonette had some of the best food he ever tasted in the country."

Former representative Marty Russo of Illinois once attended a banquet at another famous Philadelphia restaurant—but would not eat the lobster dinner because he was waiting for the banquet to be over so he could go to Shank's.

In August 2009, Shank's & Evelyn's resurfaced as Shank's Original at 120 South Fifteenth Street, with Pamela Poppa running the show. "My mother [Evelyn] sold the building," Poppa told the *Inquirer* at the time. "She wants to try Center City where it's *happening*." Everything continued to be made on premises: cheesesteaks with sirloin, sliced-to-order hoagies, the gigantic *giambotta* and the signature chicken cutlet sandwiches.

Poppa sold the Shank's name to Marcello Ciurlino around this time too, and he planned to franchise the name. A Shank's Original sandwich shop remains open along South Columbus Boulevard at Pier 40.

34

Levis Hot Dogs

Surprisingly, figuring out who invented the hot dog is seemingly difficult. For over a century, many stories have speculated on its origins, ranging from it first being served by a Caribbean immigrant, Thomas Francis Xavier Morris, who offered the bunned delight in Paterson, New Jersey, as early as 1892. Or one tale says that it was inspired by a cartoon of a dachshund in a roll drawn by *New York Evening Journal* cartoonist Tad Dorgan around 1901. Of course, the story that many Philadelphians believe to be the truth is that the sausage-on-a-bun concept was invented by Abe Levis and Anna Solo Levis, who opened a sandwich cart in South Philly in 1895.

As Levis's story went, Abraham "Abe" Levis ended up in America from Lithuania at the age of fourteen, when he was evading a draft into wartime service. He eventually married Anna Solo, and together they opened a sandwich shop in the South Street business district.

When Abe and Anna began serving their all-beef hot dogs, a nickel would buy you three of their bread-and-meat combinations—they were very clear in their positioning of the hot dogs, which were "distinct from sandwiches." Family lore says that Anna had the idea of putting frankfurters into Parker House rolls, and Abe took the initiative to order longer custom-baked rolls that better fit the sausages. Philadelphia had never seen such a combination before, making it an instant success.

Eventually, the hot dog king and queen moved their location in 1908, to 507 South Sixth Street, when the couple purchased the building and one next door for $12,500 from Nathan Snellenburger. According to an *Inquirer* report, the lot measured 20 by 120.5 feet.

Small, but packing mass appeal, Levis's menu of hot dogs, actual sandwiches, fish cakes, ice cream and homemade sodas quickly became a hot spot of Philadelphia. The hot dog remained the star along with its deluxe version: a hot dog and a fish cake on the same bun, which became casually known as the Philly Surf & Turf. (For the record, the fish cake itself became so popular that it likely reached 100 million served far before McDonald's introduced its version, and Levis's recipe would become so indispensable that by 1970 it was a corporate secret guarded by Price Waterhouse.)

As it grew in popularity, Levis Hot Dogs became the neighborhood's epicenter. "It was a place that was open all night—people hung out there," noted South Street historian Joel Spivak, who said that Levis's hot dogs and cherry sodas were legendary.

For many years, it even served as the de facto Fifth Ward Republican headquarters and a favorite spot after Little League baseball games. Abe identified the promise of cinema early after its introduction and situated a screen on his roof for folks gathered in the nearby Starr Garden to view silent movies. On summer nights, the community would gather to watch

Levis Hot Dogs stood for nearly one hundred years, headquartered between South and Lombard Streets, on Sixth Street. *Courtesy of Penn Archives.*

films projected onto a screen situated on the shop's roof. More and more locals of the working-class neighborhood turned to Levis for cheap, delicious meals, including the signature Champaign Cherry soda.

Speaking of the signature, now-iconic soda, it was brewed in the basement and sold out of Levis originally for a penny. It was a "wine-like brew" and was said to have a cider taste. According to the Champ Cherry website, in 1950, one devoted Phillies fan swore to drink a glass of the Phillies red soda each day until the team won a title. The ritual worked: after hundreds of glasses, the Phillies won the National League Pennant that very same year. In honor of the brew's magical powers, Abe changed its name from Champaign Cherry to Champ Cherry.

By the 1970s, the Levis children had opened two more Greater Philadelphia locations, though all three are now closed.

For nearly one hundred years, the family-owned mainstay headquartered on Sixth, between South and Lombard Streets, served up an all hot dog menu and Champ Cherry soda before closing its doors in 1990. Over the years, "The Combination" had evolved (known locally as previously mentioned, as the "Philly Surf 'n' Turf"), including the addition of pepper hash—the sweet-and-sour vegetable dice of cabbage, peppers and carrots. As Rick Nichols said in 2009 in the *Philadelphia Inquirer*, "It was a refreshing un-coleslaw, mayo-less and mildly vinegary, a cool contrast to fried fish, crisp and tangy, but sweet in the finish."

The "Philly Surf & Turf" artwork from Philadelphia artist Hawk Krall, originally created for the former Hot Diggity hot dog shop on South Street, as a celebration of the classic Philly combo created by Levis. *Courtesy of Hawk Krall Illustration.*

While similar, but not exact to the OG, variations popped up at Lenny's Hot Dogs in Feasterville, Moe's Hot Dogs in the city and Johnny's Hots on Delaware Avenue. Johnny's Hots' owner John Danze actually started including pepper hash on his rendition of the surf 'n' turf when an old-timer who grew up on Levis was appalled he didn't offer it and brought him the recipe.

A few of the older cheesesteak stands, including Pat's and Philip's, do continue to offer the fish cake on a hot dog roll—without the hot dog, but available smothered in onions and Cheez Whiz. For some time, if you were curious about an Italian version, Texas Wieners in deep South Philly offered an option for a fish cake with broccoli rabe and provolone. (Sadly, the iconic Texas Wieners has since closed its doors.)

The Levis lunch stand rode a trend not just in Philly but nationally as well. At the time, frankfurters and lunch carts were proliferating across the country, especially where young people and working people congregated. As seen in an 1893 clipping from the *Philadelphia Inquirer*, food carts were originally positioned as temperance aides.

The long defunct hot dog joint was forever immortalized by artist/illustrator Hawk Krall. Elliott Hirsh (of Elliott's Amazing fame) originally bought the shop before it closed in the '90s to get the rights to its Champ Cherry soda and try his hand at franchising the Levis brand.

The original location, on Sixth Street between Lombard and South Streets, closed in 1992, just shy of one hundred years. It later became home to Blackbird Pizzeria, a popular vegan restaurant.

Abe Levis was known as a visionary and hard taskmaster. Constantly smoking large cigars, Abe had 10 Rules of Behavior posted to the wall. The full list has not survived, but rule no. 10 is said to have been "Talk less, eat and drink more."

Levis Hot Dogs Recipe: Pepper Hash
Adapted from Levis recipe by Applegate Natural & Organic Meats
Makes about 6 cups

½ medium green cabbage (about 1 ¼ pounds)
½ green bell pepper
½ red bell pepper
1 carrot, peeled
¼ cup apple cider vinegar
¼ cup granulated sugar
½ teaspoon mustard seeds
½ teaspoon celery seeds
½ teaspoon salt
¼ teaspoon black pepper

Finely shred cabbage, bell peppers and carrot by hand or in a food processor. Combine in a large mixing bowl.

Combine the vinegar, sugar, mustard seeds, celery seeds, salt and pepper in a small saucepan and cook, stirring, over low heat until sugar is dissolved, about 5 minutes. Pour the hot vinegar mixture over the vegetables and toss well to coat.

Wrap tightly in plastic wrap and refrigerate for at least four hours (or overnight) for flavors to develop. For a true Philly dog experience, layer pepper hash on top of hot dog with a smashed fish and potato cake and a drizzle of brown mustard.

35

New Corned Beef Academy

1605 Walnut Street

Howard Nutinsky was a comedian. He would collect deli jokes that he could serve up when serving you a sandwich. To him, telling a good joke and giving good food went hand in hand.

A sample joke, told often by comedian Lou Holtz and recycled by Nutinsky, was this:

> *A customer kept complaining that two slices of bread with a meal weren't enough. So, the owner told the waiter to give him three slices. The man still beefed, so he given four slices, and then five. Finally, the owner had the waiter slice a giant loaf of deli rye in two, lengthwise, and serve the halves on a plate. On the way out, the customer told the owner: "The dinner was fine, but how come you went back to two slices of bread?"*

The Center City deli, which opened in the summer of 1995, was graced with light, bright, humorous posters splashed on its walls. It fit the comic owner's personality. Like the name suggested, it was the "new" version of the previous rendition of the Corned Beef Academy, previously owned by Joe Wolf, which closed in December 1990. The original was known for its fat, juicy sandwiches. But it shuttered its doors.

When it came time for Nutinsky to open his own establishment, he asked Wolf if he could use his former restaurant's name, and he consented. They had a history: prior to becoming a deli owner, Howard was a former busboy, dishwasher and sandwich-maker. His first job was at Bain's cafeteria on South Broad Street at the ripe age of fifteen, pushing a cart and cleaning tables. Eventually, he worked toward becoming the manager at the original Corned Beef Academy restaurants at Sixteenth and Sansom Streets and at Eighteenth and JFK Boulevard, clocking a twelve-year stint working alongside Wolf.

Nutinsky's rendition was said to be just as good as Wolf's, perhaps cleaner and sharper than before. Per Nutinsky's point of view, his version was "exactly the same deal as before" but with a few '90s touches applied to the menu. The signature corned beef special, clocking in at $5.45, was piled high and more than enough for a hungry diner. Roast turkey sandwiches were carved warm, right from the bird. The chef's salad towered with fresh ham and turkey. You could even get a three-egg omelet until 10:00 a.m., punched with generous pieces of corned beef.

The Jewish deli became a hot spot for visiting athletes and celebrities to fuel up before a big game or show. Before a show at the Merriam, Jackie Mason would indulge in a lunch of Jewish soul food. Tennis champ Pete Sampras loved to tear up a corned beef special in his day. Basketball Olympic gold medalist Dawn Staley enjoyed chowing down on a tuna fish salad sandwich on rye bread. The former Sixers great Bill Cunningham enjoyed plenty of egg salad sandwiches on black bread with a birch beer in his day.

When lines became long, Nutinsky would serve customers free trays of French fries to keep them happy until their turn to order.

"Corned Beef Academy is your kind of place," wrote *Inquirer*'s Elaine Tait. "Good breads, thick fillings and a brisk turnover make the Academy a popular eat-in or take-out spot with center-city business community."

"In my opinion, they were one of the best Jewish style deli restaurants in Center City (at least since Marty's Cafeteria closed about 10 years ago)," wrote the late Holly Moore. "This is just what the name implies, and the smell of corned beef and roast brisket is mouthwatering. Lawyers and businessmen in the neighborhood ignore the non-décor for the thick sandwiches."

After more than a decade of slinging hearty sandwiches, Nutinsky pivoted his career into real estate, and eventually the sandwich shop closed.

36

Jimmy's Milan

39 South Nineteenth Street

What lives on from the erstwhile supper club at Nineteenth and Chestnut Streets is its namesake salad. The Milan was confidently retro in a time when Sinatra was in his prime. It started with chopped crunchy iceberg lettuce generously tossed with a tangy-sweet dressing that was one part Thousand Island and one part Italian, with a splash of Worcestershire. Topped with chopped tomato, crispy bacon, quartered hard-cooked egg and fresh chilled and peeled shrimp, it was all the fun of a BLT, plus shrimp. It quickly became a Philly classic that was capable of satisfying salad lovers for decades.

"It was a nice big salad with lots of shrimp, and it was cold and hearty. Just an iconic Philadelphia salad," reminisced Chris Scarduzio to *Philly Magazine* in 2009, citing his father for introducing it to him. He loved it so much that he pulled from the Jimmy's Milan archives to add a riff on the salad to his menu at the now-defunct Table 31.

You can find the Milan, with slight modifications and name changes, at restaurants like Cotoletta, in Bala Cynwyd and Fitler Square; Villa di Roma in South Philadelphia; and D'Angelo's in Rittenhouse Square—which is actually where Jimmy's Milan chef Tony D'Angelo still works and tosses it together.

Even better, the legacy lives on through Ann Conlin—whose late husband, Jimmy DiBattista, was the son of the restaurant's founder. Conlin bottled up

Jimmy Milan's supperclub became iconic for its namesake salad and its signature dressing, which continues to be mass produced by the founder's family. *Courtesy of Philly's Original Milan Salad Dressing.*

the dressing that makes the Milan really what it is and sells it at Philadelphia-area grocery stores, and online, at milan39.com.

But beyond the iconic salad, the moody Jimmy's Milan was an institution. Let's start from the beginning…

WHEN JIMMY DEBATTISTA BOUGHT THE Milan in 1951, he simply added "Jimmy's" to the name so he wouldn't have to take down the existing restaurant's sign. The Milan itself was risqué for postwar Philadelphia, a piano bar that attracted sexy singles and catered to Philadelphia's sports stars and starlets. It was famous for its discretion, given that certain individuals from South Philadelphia would arrive on certain evenings with girlfriends and on others with their wives. It became famous for its steak-and-a-half dinner options, where you would be served a prime sirloin fit for dinner alone with a side of baked ziti, asparagus and the notorious Milan Salad. It was Jimmy who added the famous bowl of iceberg lettuce to the menu.

Locals also loved the down-home Italian dish giambotta, a legendary plate of scrambled eggs with peppers, sliced potatoes, grilled onions and sausage that was consumed late at night by those who flocked to the lounge-lizard scene until the '90s.

Waitresses were known as the "Milan Girls," the restaurant went by "Pasta Palace" to many and the location became known as an old-school politico haunt, where you'd easily pick up political flavor on the city any night of the week. Jimmy's was often billed as a place that "had enough character to provoke conversation."

Jimmy DeBattista founded Jimmy's Milan in 1951. He simply added "Jimmy's" to the name so he wouldn't have to take down the existing restaurant's sign, which read "Milan." *Courtesy of Philly's Original Milan Salad Dressing.*

Owner Jimmy DiBatista Sr. died in 1973 at the age of fifty-two of a heart attack. Though he had passed, the restaurant and his salad lived on—and continued to—for decades.

In 1976, in the *Philadelphia Inquirer*, Bill Curry said South Philadelphia mayor Mike Goffredo claimed that Jimmy's Milan had the best veal dishes in the city.

In the summer of 1993, after forty years, Jimmy's Milan closed its doors and filed for bankruptcy. On December 6, 1993, the restaurant reopened with a new owner, Al Hutkin, whose claim to fame was running Crazy Albert's in New Hope in the '80s. Hutkin continued to serve the same menu and even employed Jimmy's son after the restaurant purchase.

Eventually, the Milan closed once its chef Tony D'Angelo went off to open his namesake restaurant, D'Angelo's, at Twentieth Street, where he continued to honor and serve the Milan salad (though now named after himself).

Jimmy Milan's Recipe: Milan Salad
As told to *Philadelphia Inquirer*
by longtime Jimmy's Milan chef Tony D'Angelo.
Serves 2

2 tablespoons mayonnaise
1 teaspoon ketchup
1 teaspoon Worcestershire sauce
2 teaspoons sweet pickle relish
Chopped iceberg and romaine lettuce
1 hard-cooked egg, coarsely chopped
2 tablespoons baby shrimp
1 ripe plum tomato, cubed
3 tablespoons crumbled fried bacon

Combine mayo, ketchup, Worcestershire sauce and sweet pickle relish for dressing. On a plate, top lettuce with all ingredients but bacon. Toss. Scatter with bacon and enjoy.

PART VIII

SOUTH PHILLY ITALIAN KINGPINS

37
Palumbo's

Eighth and Catherine Streets

Palumbo's was a symbol of what South Philadelphia used to be. Sunday nights, more than two hundred locals would flood to the supper club, eating plates of penne rigatoni while watching impersonators sing Frank Sinatra songs.

The real Sinatra once sang there too, in 1946 for a Red Cross fundraiser. And he came back many times later, courting Ava Gardner over plates of spaghetti and clams.

It was a landmark that dominated an entire block for more than 110 years, billed as "America's oldest nightclub." But before it was a neighborhood restaurant meets nightclub, it was a boardinghouse catering to newly arrived Italian immigrants. It was founded by Antonio Palumbo, a tailor from Abruzzo, in 1884 at Eighth and Catherine Streets. When immigrants arrived on the docks off of Washington Avenue, they spoke zero English and had tags pinned to their clothes that read "Palumbo's," helping to set them off on the right path in their new land.

There, they would pay ninety cents a week to live and for all the spaghetti they could eat until they could find work elsewhere, for the local railroads, mines or garment factories.

"So many Italian immigrants came to Palumbo's that federal officials began to suspect it was a padrone system that was exploiting the immigrants," reported the *Philadelphia Inquirer*. A U.S. immigration official, Agent Adrian Bonnelly, was actually dispatched in 1912 to investigate, and what he found was that a "group of Italian American businessmen had banded together to aid, comfort and assist the[ir] brethren." The agent befriended the Palumbo family, and thus started a lifelong friendship.

There was a line of three Frank Palumbos who ran the Palumbo's show through the years. The second, Antonio's grandson Frank Palumbo Sr., started his Palumbo's ambitions at the ripe age of thirteen, cutting onions in the kitchen. During the '30s and '40s, he'd take thousands of neighborhood kids to the ballpark or zoo, and his philanthropy was widely publicized by the reporters who joined him often at the restaurant to eat and drink for free.

His claim to fame though was when he transformed Palumbo's into a multi-building banquet hall and entertainment complex built out of twenty rowhouses and a funeral parlor. Every time he acquired a new rowhouse, he would knock down the wall between the last. He did it without permits, and no city official would dare to bother Frank about that.

In Palumbo's mid-twentieth century heyday, the food and entertainment made it a premier destination for parties, weddings, reunions and other milestone celebrations, especially for Philadelphia's Italian Americans. It was also a popular gathering spot for the city's politicians and civic leaders.

Frank Palumbo Sr. was seen as unattainable. He lived in a mansion on the Main Line and even installed running water in his daughter's dollhouse. He was the "mayor" of Palumbo's, mingling nightly with regulars, handing out gold watches, bottles of expensive perfume and even the tie around his neck, according to the *Inquirer* in 1995.

His club was cited as having the longest bar in the world—478 feet long to be exact. It was so popularized that a newspaper said it was "lavish enough to inspire envy from Gotham to Hollywood."

One of his claims to fame was his annual Valentine's Day dance, where he'd host the couples who were married in the club the year before, serving

Palumbo's was a premier destination for Philadelphia's Italian Americans to celebrate special occasions, like Richard Buono had in 1943. *Courtesy of the Historical Society of Pennsylvania.*

Palumbo's Frank Palumbo eating spaghetti with Frank Sinatra during the height of the restaurant's popularity in the '50s. *Courtesy of the* Philadelphia Inquirer.

them filet mignons and bottles of champagne on the house. (At the height of Palumbo's popularity in the 1940s, Frank was touted to be the world's largest purchaser of champagne.)

It was around the '70s when Palumbo's started to experience a downhill battle. Atlantic City casinos were on the rise, stealing the high-level talent from the club that drew in the crowds.

Frank Sr. passed in 1983 at the age of seventy-two. Rumor had it that on his death bed, he offered the paramedics dinner. His son Frank Jr.—known affectionately as "the kid"—took over after his father's passing. Then a forty-year-old lawyer educated at Villanova and Widener Universities, he did his part to improve Palumbo's but lacked the passion for the family business. Things became lax; employees began to steal from him.

If Philadelphia ever had an inferiority complex about its restaurants, it was Frank Jr.'s mission to overcome it. He had multiple institutions by the time he took over—the Nostalgia Room, two banquet halls, Palumbo's and Club Revel (known as the CR Club).

In May 1993, Frank had enough and approached Esposito Inc. for help, an Italian Market meat purveyor that attributed 20 percent of its business to the social club. But in the '90s, Frank was behind on his bills to Esposito, so he cut them in on his business by selling them Palumbo's banquet hall.

Frank's team continued to run the show until the very end. Albert "Al" D'Angelo was the chef for more than thirty years, making the tomato sauce just like how the Palumbo sisters had when four of them ran the kitchen for the first half of the twentieth century. Simmered in a sixty-gallon stainless-steel kettle, it was made of veal and pork, onions, celery, carrots and seasonings like butter, bay leaf, basil, rosemary, salt and pepper. The famous sauce covered plates of gnocchi, an Al staple, and they always carried fresh-baked Sarcone's loaves.

In 1994, a devasting fire erupted at Palumbo's, taking 120 firefighters to get the fire under control. *Courtesy of Old Images of Philadelphia.*

On June 20, 1994, following a South Philadelphia Lioness Club meeting, a fire erupted. It took 120 firefighters an hour and fifty minutes to get the fire under control, reported the *Inquirer.*

There was no insurance on the building. There were no fire alarms in the building. Rumors speculated that it was Frank Jr. who torched the place, but as reported in local newspapers, it was in 1992 that he dropped a $7,000-a-year policy for $600,000 of fire insurance. Because of the fire, seventy full- and part-time employees lost their jobs, more than twenty living in the direct neighborhood. Local businesses, such as Anthony "Lu-Lu" Lucchesi's Fish Market, suffered from Palumbo's being sold, too, as the social club was their biggest customer.

In August 1994, a demolition crew began to knock down the Palumbo's Nostalgia Room and banquet hall. Neighbors and former employees lined up to watch it firsthand. The CR Room remained intact, but over time, burglars looted its remains—including more than $5,000 worth of booze. Eventually, the CR Club caught fire too, on August 25, 1994. And then, on September 10, 1994, an arsonist set fire to the remains. (Palumbo's experienced five fires over the span of three months.)

In January 1995, Palumbo's and Esposito ended their gentleman's agreement by selling the property. Eventually, a Rite-Aid Pharmacy called the location home.

Palumbo's legion remains as the unspoken center of South Philadelphia's golden age. "If you wanted to run for office in South Philadelphia, you went to see your ward leaders, of course," recalled City Councilman Frank DiCicco to the *Inquirer.* "But Frank Palumbo was really the guy you had to see. You went there to seek his blessing. You did your fundraisers there. He gave you a great price—you couldn't beat the deal."

38

Strolli's

1528 Dickinson Street

In 1912, John Strolli opened a taproom in South Philadelphia. A year earlier, his wife gave birth to their son, John D. Strolli, in the upper floors of Palumbo's Restaurant, which doubled as a boardinghouse. When John D.'s father became ill in 1938, he pivoted his career from teaching music to taking over his father's business, transforming the taproom into a restaurant.

John D. was determined to make the restaurant work, even if they had to starve. He was committed to luring locals with good food at low prices, and he stuck by that for the restaurant's full lifespan. (The secret to keeping the prices down through the years was, as Strolli's wife, Carmela, confessed to the *Inquirer*, having a big family and putting them to work. Carmela was the cook with her daughter and grandchildren helping her in the kitchen, and her son tended bar, with her niece pitching in occasionally.)

His love of music carried into the restaurant, where he would entertain patrons by strolling around his linoleum tile–lined restaurant with his beloved mandolin. On birthdays, he'd serenade his special guest with "Happy Birthday," and at closing, he'd pluck out the tune "Good Night, Ladies." John made it a tradition that he greeted every single customer as they walked in the door and sat in one of his red table-topped seats. And he and his wife served dinner every night until nine o'clock—not a second later.

John loved to swap stories with his clientele as a stogie was in his hand. A favorite of his was when Isaac Stern, an acclaimed violinist, would storm over to his restaurant after a performance at the Academy of Music. Sometimes Strolli and Stern would even bust out a duet in the restaurant.

It wasn't until the late '70s that the restaurant even got itself a sign out front. And it was listed in the phone book only under John's name, within the "tavern" yellow pages. (The phone book was an error, but John said it wasn't worth the hassle to change.) The entrance was even an adventure, with the original bar entrance blocked off when it transitioned to a restaurant in the '60s, causing guests to enter through the alley-like former ladies' entrance off of Mole Street. It was almost a mystery how so many Philadelphians discovered the restaurant in all its old-saloon aura grandeur, especially as it was practically invisible and built around word of mouth.

Arlene Notoro Morgan, *Philadelphia Inquirer* reporter in the '80s, suggested Strolli's was special because its food was "'like home' and the next-best thing to Mom's dinner table." The pastas were homemade and plump. Carmela made fresh pasta dishes like her hand-cut gnocchi or ravioli, which were light puffs full of creamy ricotta cheese. Her chicken parmigiana and veal piccata were well-pounded, generally drenched with their flavorful sauces, delightfully seasoned and so huge you'd never be able to finish in one seating.

One notable bargain in the '80s was a filet mignon with a side salad and spaghetti for a mere $7.00. Even better, then you could get stuff eggplant parmigiana for $2.50.

Eventually, John retired and turned over the business to his daughter, Phyllis Seiple. Even after retiring, he couldn't help himself, frequenting the restaurant and visiting with the regulars he came to know so well. In the late '80s, John's son, Michael Strolli, expanded the business outside the city, to Chester Pike in Eddystone.

In 1993, John Strolli passed. Maria Donato, a longtime friend, shared in the *Philadelphia Daily News* that it was common for people to hear about the restaurant's homemade pasta and its mandolin-playing host.

PART IX

ICONIC STEAKHOUSE CHARM

39

Arthur's

Originally at 216 Chancellor Street; Relocated to 1512 Walnut Street

In 1986, one of Philadelphia's oldest, most well-known restaurants, Arthur's, closed its doors. Operating for more than fifty years—fifty-four, to be exact—since 1932, the classic steakhouse thrived well before the arrival of chains like Morton's, the Palm and Ruth's Chris.

Arthur's was owned and named after Arthur Effron, a shy, kind man who introduced his namesake restaurant in a tiny rowhouse on Chancellor Street that was once home to America's first professional novelist, Charles Brockden Brown. The business started on a shoestring budget, with a borrowed stove from Arthur's mother-in-law that was missing one of its legs, and the first day's receipts totaled thirty cents. Those days, he had two tables, eight chairs and a tub filled with ice that served as a fridge. It began as a twenty-four-hour business and attracted a wide range of clientele, from dock workers and produce hucksters to journalists, pub-crawlers and even show-business folks who stopped by during the early hours of the morning before they were off to work.

Arthur was never fazed by celebrities frequenting his spot. One story went that a waiter came rushing to the kitchen to announce that the famous conductor Leopold Stokowski had walked in. In reply, Arthur was supposed to have responded with, "Don't get excited. He can only eat one steak."

In the '30s, the restaurant was known for its reasonable prices. For example, you'd be able to get yourself a generous steak sandwich, complete with fries, pickles, celery and a coffee, for forty-five cents. In 1942, Effron decided to take his first vacation since opening, to Atlantic City. His namesake restaurant caught fire, and Effron vowed to never take another vacation.

Until World War II, Arthur's sirloin steaks sold for one dollar and came with rye bread, potatoes and a big dish of onions and tomatoes. In 1960, development of Society Hill closed the restaurant and moved it to Walnut Street. Effron was not overly impressed with the new, more elegant space, as it was "too fancy" for his taste and left the front of the house to his two children to run.

For one, the Center City location was much larger. The Old Key Bar was a popular rendezvous spot for those in town, known as a place to be seen for the in crowd.

In 1964, the founder passed, leaving the restaurant to his wife, Rose. Eventually, following Rose's passing, her daughter, Shirley Kahn, and her husband, Herman, took over the business. Nineteen years later in 1983, after a series of successes like opening his own restaurant and bar in the Warwick Hotel called Elan, Shirley's brother, Gene, returned to the family business to help his sister

Shirley, in an interview with the *Philadelphia Inquirer*, suggested that old-time family restaurants like theirs survive because "there is a certain caring you develop from having been raised in the business, from knowing it as a child. There is the involvement and the pride that comes from the knowledge that you are continuing something started by your parents."

In a full-page ad published in 1968, Arthur's allowed customers to "go behind the scenes" to better understand the "high standard of quality" and care the owners' put into sourcing their menu. Co-owner Herman Kahn was shown hand-selecting the prime ribs that would later be served next to a photo of a coffee testing that helped develop the restaurant's signature blend of coffee. It also showed the restaurant's daily selection of "ocean-fresh" seafood—which was hand-selected like the beef—and the quality dairy products they sourced.

For Arthur's fiftieth anniversary celebration in 1982, the Kahns created a special souvenir menu, dressed in Prohibition-era costumes and hosted big bands all week, as well as a '30s-themed fashion show. *Inquirer* columnist John Corr joked at the time, "Without doubt, Arthur would have thought everyone was making entirely too much fuss about the occasion."

Over time, Arthur's had internal union problems. In 1984, twenty-five of its workers went on strike and started a picket line that lasted eleven weeks in front of the restaurant. It remained open the entire time. Up until 1985, Arthur's was Philadelphia's only restaurant specializing in

Arthur's Steak House advertisement, as featured in the *Philadelphia Inquirer* in 1968. *Courtesy of the* Philadelphia Inquirer.

top-quality steaks and chops. Patrons not only appreciated the perfectly cooked-to-temp steaks that they could select from a window meat display case but also the baskets of high-quality breads and the garlicky pickles on every table.

In July 1986, the siblings decided to close Arthur's in order to pursue other interests. The closing came with speculation that it was the end of the steakhouse era—as American tastes changed, so did the demand for a big steak dinner. However, soon after came a new steakhouse, Arturo's, backed by Giuseppe Giuliani, serving similar mesquite-grilled steak and chop entrées, as well as Italian specialties and seafood.

Interesting enough, Giuliani, a Pisa, Italy native, worked at Arthur's from 1961 to 1972, and over time, he developed a close friendship with Arthur himself. "He told him that, 'if I worked hard, I would one day have my own restaurant in America,'" Giuliani relayed to the *Philadelphia Inquirer* prior to his opening. "Neither of us ever dreamed that I would one day own Arthur's."

Soon after, Susanna Foo took over Arthur's location for her acclaimed namesake restaurant, which had a successful twenty-five-year run, closing in 2009.

40

Frankie Bradley's

1320 Chancellor Street

In September 1933, Frankie Bradley's restaurant opened its doors at the corner of Juniper and Chancellor Streets in Center City. It was named after its owner, Frank Bloch, who is of Jewish heritage and was born and raised in South Philadelphia.

But before he became a restauranteur, he was a storied '20s prizefighter. When he was young, Frankie contributed to the family's slim income by peddling papers on the corner of Fifteenth and Market Streets—where he'd have to use his fists to defend his territory. As he toughened up, he started to get intertwined into the local fight club scene, changing his name to "Frankie Bradley"—adopting an Irish name during the World War I era was almost the mandatory thing to do (the sport was then dominated by the Irish). "Even the Italian boys changed their names," recalled Frankie to the *Philadelphia Daily News* in 1972.

He became so successful in the ring that he fought in two world championships in the bantamweight division. Lacking the killer knockout punch that would allow him to be a champion, he pivoted into the restaurant business. Years later, it was reported that it was Joe Fox, onetime British boxing champion, who "jabbed" Frankie into the restaurant business. Frankie first opened a tiny luncheonette at Juniper and Filbert, now the site of a city hall annex. Soon he was making moves: to a larger luncheonette on North Broad Street and then to his first deluxe restaurant, The Food Nest, on South Broad Street, which launched during Prohibition. (As record stood, like many others, he was selling illegal booze from under the counter, and he got raided more than once.) His next move was to South Juniper Street, between Locust and Spruce, a place he called The Romanian Inn. And then, he moved once more, for good, to the final home of Frankie Bradley's on Chancellor Street (known affectionately as the "little street" below Walnut, at Juniper).

Ever since Frankie began his culinary career, celebrities followed to all of his locations. He decorated his restaurant with photos of famous people who dined there. From Dick Clark, Eddie Fisher and Elizabeth Taylor, plus many, many more, Frankie Bradley's quickly became and maintained its reputation as a "show-biz" spot—especially those connected to theater—where you'd want to be seen or go for the people watching. Many actors considered it the "Sardis of Philadelphia," and like the original Sardis, its customer base came from many walks of life.

In the kitchen, though, it was the Jewish recipes for matzo ball and kreplach soups, gefilte fish, rib steak with garlic and potato pancakes that guests coveted. While his name changed to Irish descent, his menu stayed true to his heritage and served true ethnic origins of Jewish soul food. There were less authentic options at the steakhouse, such as large jumbo shrimp cocktail, Caesar salad, veal picante, and surf and turf, but every meal came with a bowl of sauerkraut and dill pickles and tomatoes to stay true to the experience Frankie wanted.

Frankie Bradley, always found nestled away in one of his restaurant's booths, worked well into his late seventies, passing in 1976 at the ripe age of eighty-one. In his farewell, the *Philadelphia Daily News* praised his personality and charisma, noting him as one of Philadelphia's "most colorful characters" and that "a little bit of Philadelphia's heart vanished when Frankie Bradley died." It also reported that garlic, dill and hot pepper were the loves of his life—which many were aware of from his use of free-flowing garlic—and his biggest regret was that he could never figure out how to successfully (read: deliciously) put garlic into ice cream and make it edible.

The restaurant continued on under the direction of his son, Harold Bloch, and his daughter, Dorothy Adler, for another decade until they introduced managing partners from the firm Maddra Investors in 1984. Eventually, things went sour with the new partners, and they ousted Adler. In response, she took them to court. In a few short months, the partners put the restaurant up for sale in August 1986, citing it was not in response to the continued influx of tough competition over the years—they had been doing just fine—but rather the challenges of running a restaurant with several "absentee partners."

Not long after the closure, in 1987, Bradley's reopened as Hesch's (a Yiddish version of Harry) by the new owner, Harry Jay Katz. He had the original 1937 Frankie Bradley's menu and made it his mission to celebrate the tradition of the institution by bringing back "garlic steaks and seltzer bottles on the table…serving all the stuff cardiologists warn you against." His menu included chopped liver, kreplach soup, matzo-ball soup, prime meats, ribs and all big steaks. "I'm sick and tired of *nouvelle cuisine*," Katz told the *Philadelphia Inquirer* in late 1986 prior to his opening. "Bring back the red meat. Give me heartburn—please."

Eventually, Hesch's ran its course. However, what came in 2015 was a bit of the unexpected. Mark Bee, who owns N3rd and Silk City in the Northern Liberties neighborhood of Philadelphia, decided to revive the old back-street steakhouse, as Frankie Bradley's with a slight spelling change (as suggested by his lawyer). Bee subsequently spent time at Hesch's and Sisters, the city's longest-serving lesbian bar that filled the space after Hesch's. Now he was back with his version of Franky Bradley's. The location was what they dubbed an "American medieval" bar and restaurant, with a nightclub upstairs. "It's a 'house of weird,'" he's been known to say. It is anything but a replica of the original, but you can certainly take in some interesting people-watching at the reincarnation.

41

The Palm

200 South Broad Street

In 1989, The Palm in the nineteen-story Bellevue hotel building opened its doors. The longtime power lunch landmark in Center City was best known for the caricatures of celebrities adorning its walls and for having deals made over steaks. Well, it was never as much about its steak as it was about its go there to be seen hype, a frequent destination for lawyers, politicians and real estate kingpins.

The tradition of A-, B- and C- list celebs on its walls dated back to the first Palm, in New York City, where you could have found newspapermen (i.e., celebrities of their time) on the walls. That first location opened in 1926, with more than twenty to follow across the United States and with two international destinations in Mexico City. The Philadelphia location was the twelfth, lined extensively with 140 seats; in its early days, patrons needed to nab a Saturday reservation two to three weeks in advance.

Oh, and who of Philadelphia's who's who made the cut to be first sketched on the restaurant's walls? You had to be a regular. That was political drama in itself, with rumors spiraling that those selected were only Democrats, and the "giant of politics" at the time, Frank Rizzo, did not make the cut. Following some backlash, Rizzo's sketch was ordered and conveniently placed next to his lead adversary, Senator Vincent J. Fumo.

Some wannabe insiders even tried to bribe The Palm to get their picture on the wall, from $1,000 to furnishing the manager's new baby's nursery,

The Palm's Philadelphia destination became known for its caricatures, ranging from notable athletes and politicians to city pacesetters and even fictional movie characters, like Rocky Balboa. *Courtesy of the* Philadelphia Inquirer.

paying for car maintenance for a year for him or offering up their daughter for a date.

At first it was 200 caricatures. Then 350. Within a year of being opened, it climbed toward its limit of 2,000.

In 1990, the *Philadelphia Inquirer* reported The Palm was "fast becoming Philadelphia's hottest power shop." It was said to have gained its popularity practically overnight, drawing quickly a heavy political crowd. In fact, it was in close proximity to the former Hunt Room, a popular destination for half a century for many political players and business types. "You could go there and be relatively assured you would run into people you hoped to talk to," reminisced Tony May, then the executive director of the state Democratic committee, to the *Inquirer.*

However, The Palm was everything the Hunt Room was not. It had windows that opened and salads on the menu next to the steaks, as well as much less smoke and much more women. It kept up, at least at first, with the times.

Lunchtime, in particular, was a show, as jacketed waiters had to frequently dodge the networking, be-seen table-hoppers. In one corner, you'd have a district attorney, or a mayoral candidate, another councilmen and senators. Its nighttime business faded quickly after happy hour, as Philadelphia's most powerful had to get home to the kids.

It was the maître d's job to seat the powerful appropriately, which was tricky business with some people who couldn't sit next to each other, or sued one another, relayed one-time general manager Jeffrey Phillips. "Most people liked to sit by their pictures," he shared. "Especially if they're with a guest or a client." He was encouraged to remember first names of the powerful and make them feel welcome. "One of my biggest jobs [was] to make sure we [became] part of the city."

As The Palm's original history told, it exclusively sold Italian food until its owners Pio Bozzi and John Ganzi started requesting steak on the menu. To make them happy, the chefs would run to a nearby butcher shop each time the request came in, until they permanently added steak to the menu.

Philadelphia's Palm closed from time to time for renovations. It never seemed to regain its footing after a closing of more than a year, from March 2016 to July 2017, that gave it a smaller footprint and removed it from the landmark building's lobby.

In 2019, the family-run company backing The Palm filed for bankruptcy following a dispute among family members over royalties. Then in February 2020, Landry's restaurant collection, which comprises other competitive steakhouses, including Del Frisco's and Morton's, bought The Palm out of bankruptcy. Two weeks later, in early March 2020, it opted to close The Palm.

PART X

THE MOST MEMORABLE BAKERIES

AND DESSERT DARLING

42

Hesh's Éclair Bake Shoppe

7721 Castor Avenue

In 1959, Harry "Hesh" Braverman introduced his namesake kosher bakery along Castor Avenue, one that would become iconic to the greater Philadelphia region for a lighter-than-air, possibly the "world's greatest" chocolate-chip pound cake.

The Northeast Philadelphia institution, located in the residential neighborhood of Rhawnhurst, operated for fifty-four years. As the story went, Hesh tried his hand at baking after his time in World War II and following his discharge from the army. After a brief stint after the war employed as a machinist, he gave up that job to work for his sister at her bakery. There, he learned and honed his baking craft before going off on his own.

But it wasn't just chocolate-chip pound cake that everyone was after—though many were. Hesh also specialized in French eclairs, butter cookies, doughnuts, dipped macaroons and traditional kosher products like fresh loves of challah, babka, onion pockets, rugalach, crumb-topped pastries and cheese danishes.

On Saturdays, it became a tradition for locals to line up, with lines spilling into the street of those looking to collect their weekly loot of fresh-baked treats for the week. Hesh's also became a staple for special occasions for local families and at synagogues, at bar and bat mitzvahs and holiday parties.

Eventually, in 1979, Hesh retired, and the bakery changed hands from the Bravermans to Bill and Sharon Krodthoff. They owned the bakery for two decades, until it closed at the beginning of 2014. After the Krodthoffs took over, everything about the place remained, from the recipes to the sign.

Hesh's Éclair Bake Shoppe, a Northeast Philadelphia institution, operated for fifty-four years in the residential neighborhood of Rhawnhurst. *Courtesy of Jewish Exponent.*

The bakery's mashgiach—the rabbi who regularly inspected the premises for its kosher certification—for the last legs of its life was Rabbi Dov Lerner. He provided kosher supervision for the bakery for roughly twelve years. He said he was shocked at the sudden closing of the bakery in 2014, suggesting the closure left a void in many sweet-loving hearts.

For many years, Hesh's was one of the most popular kosher bakeries along Castor and Bustleton Avenues; it accompanied the city's Jewish migration north out of Logan, South Philadelphia, Strawberry Mansion, West Oak Lane and Wynnefield. But with changing demographics and the rise of supermarket bakery departments, kosher bakeries began to drop off one by one, no longer fitting the narrative of Lower Northeast Philadelphia. However, no other achieved a cult following like Hesh's, even earning a Facebook group ("Save Hesh's") built for loyal customers to share their personal stories about their love for Hesh's and rally together to bring back the beloved bakery.

Harold Messinger, a hazzan at Congregation Beth Am Israel in Penn Valley, reminisced for the *Jewish Exponent* that he

> *regularly stopped into the bakery for challah, at least two chocolate chip loafs and maybe a rye bread. As a kid, you always knew that you weren't leaving empty-handed. You were guaranteed at least one melt-in-your mouth cookie: something with neon-blue sprinkles or dark chocolate sprinkles or the most magical of all, the multicolored sprinkled cookie.*

Speaking of the famous chocolate-chip loaf, he confessed that it was something of a miracle, "so many, many chocolate chips crammed into a lighter-than-air loaf that was as good in my mind's eye as it was in real life." In his household, it was known as "The Disappearing Cake" for how quickly it would be down to its last crumb.

"It was something more than just eggs, flour, sugar and a bajillion chocolate chips. Hesh's sifted in a healthy measure of love—consistently and deliciously, from the time I was a kid until the time my own kids were old enough to appreciate a good piece of cake," continued Messinger.

Longtime Hesh's customer Helen Fanning grew up in Rhawnhurst and shared that her family would go to the neighborhood bakery for doughnuts on Sunday, for birthday cakes to graduation cakes. She even recalled snacking on butter cookies on the way home from school as a girl, and later, when Fanning had her first child, a friend brought Hesh's cookies to the hospital.

"I don't think there was an event we didn't have Hesh's at the table," Fanning shared with the *Philadelphia Inquirer*.

Another repeat patron, Kris McCourt, said the butter cookies were "out of this world" and "always seemed to make her feel better when she was sick." McCourt's daughter got her wedding cake there too. "It was a small bakery. It was in the area. Had a great reputation," said McCourt. She also always got her father a strawberry shortcake from Hesh's for his birthday.

"What are we going to do for Dad's birthday?" she asked following the 2014 closing.

For those not lucky enough to experience Hesh's, Philadelphia lawyer Helen Braverman—whose father-in-law was the bakery's founder, Hesh—told the *Philadelphia Inquirer* that she and his son, David, managed to pry the chocolate-chip pound cake recipe from Hesh, who died in 1998. (Hesh hadn't shared before because he did not want David and Helen to go into the business.)

"When he finally did turn [the recipe] over, it was for a 250-pound batch. Try breaking that down!" said Helen. "And, even worse, the recipe called for 'secret stuff.'" Not to worry though, when handing over the recipe, Hesh provided them with a large plastic take-out food container that was hand-labeled across the top with "Secret Stuff."

Since then, she's discovered what the "Secret Stuff" was but promised to keep it in the family. She did tease loyal Hesh's fans: "Who knows, maybe somewhere down the line I will take the secret stuff and bring Hesh's chocolate chip loaf back to life."

Over time, some nearby bakeries have advertised having the recipe. At Fishers Tudor House in Bensalem, one baker that had trained under Hesh admitted to knowing and using the recipe. The bakery even admits that Braverman helped set up their bakery. However, Fishers used shaved chocolate rather than actual chips, and the cake was more yellow and dense. It's close to but not a replica of the famed original.

43

Rindelaub's Bakery & Coffee Shop

From the 1950s to the early 1980s, Carl Rindelaub perfected the German chocolate cake in his small-time namesake bakery near Rittenhouse Square. The bakery, with a street-level storefront and antique second-story kitchen, was the creator of four honest layers of light and moist chocolate cake nestled with buttery, semisweet fudge.

Not to confuse Rindelaub's rendition of German chocolate cake with the confection invented by Samuel German in 1957 for Baker's baking-chocolate company, in which the icing is made of coconut and chopped pecans. Neither of those toppings were present in *this* German chocolate cake, which was coated in a fine exterior of cake crumbs. (Lilla Milewski, an employee of the bakery for five years, suggested "German" was attached to the name presumably because of the owner's German heritage.)

The famed cake's recipe didn't actually originate from Rindelaub, but it might as well have been. As legend has it, a German American man named "Fricke," who had baked in the navy, reluctantly handed the recipe over to Rindelaub after a period of time holding it very close to his chest.

Eventually, Rindelaub taught Bill Meyers, who headed the kitchen for forty-five years, starting as a dishwasher.

The interesting twist to the beloved Rindelaub cake shop is that it only resided in its Rittenhouse building until the 1980s, when Rindelaub regrettably sold his building just a few years before he passed. The original home was a testament to its time, lined with fudge kettles and tray ovens, and used a dumbwaiter to carry down completed cakes from the second floor to the bakery's store. The bakery's building was placed on Philadelphia's historic register in 1995. In the bakery's heyday, local street signs designated the block the "French Quarter" to draw attention to its charming, village-like string of shops.

However, the Rindelaub's legacy continued. Barry Brodie leased the iconic storefront and continued to sell its iconic desserts, from the German chocolate cake to cinnamon buns.

In a *Philadelphia Inquirer* interview in 2001, Brodie suggested that the famous cake recipe was so sacred that "Bill [Meyers] had the German chocolate cake in his head." (It was noted though that Brodie's son Evan eventually learned his way through the recipe and perfected re-creating it.)

Brodie also shared that he hated seeing the baking history end, but he vowed to never change the German chocolate cake, "made precisely the way Carl Rindelaub bequeathed it into Bill Meyers' head." Brodie continued to carry on the Rindelaub's name.

Through its time, the cake became a neighborhood icon, a mainstay at locals' birthday parties and holidays and a repeat order for weddings, even those posher ones at the Four Seasons Hotel. It became so popular that he was having to keep up with the demand of baking 350 or more every single week. (The price point was even hard to beat—a cake that served six priced out at eleven dollars.) The busiest day every year was the day before Thanksgiving, as folks stocked up on sweet supplies for their family dinners.

Middleweight contender Kevin Tillman was known to eat a slice of Rindelaub's chocolate cake before every match and had done so for years.

It wasn't just a special-occasion or celebrity-sighting bakery either. Long lines of businesspeople would form every morning for their coffee and jelly doughnuts. The street itself became known as "Rindelaub's" Row because of the bakery.

In 2001, the Brodie family was forced out of the original location by developers and moved into a new, cramped shop across the street from the original location. The space was two thousand square feet smaller and was not equipped with baking facilities on site or restaurant space. They did, however, have a baking facility in Northeast Philadelphia, and they'd truck down cakes, cookies and pies on a daily basis. The new location was so small that the family would have to turn people away.

In December 2002, after six decades in business, Rindelaub's closed its doors in Rittenhouse. Evan Brodie expressed to the *Philadelphia Inquirer*, "We couldn't do it any longer." His mother, Marlene, ran the store with two helpers, but after a back surgery, she was physically unable to do so, and the family was stretched thin. (In addition to the Rittenhouse location, they had the bakery in the Northeast at 7364 Frankford Avenue, and Evan also owned the Park South Diner on Nineteenth Street and the 401 Diner in Conshohocken.)

Their last day of business was on Thanksgiving Eve, when they produced 2,600 pies, 1,000 less than normal due to their space limitations.

Locals cried out over the closure, reminiscing about what the bakery meant to them. "Every time we had an occasion, we'd go there....We'd even make up occasions like grandparents' day or 'coming home from college day,'" shared Dee Kaplan to the *Philadelphia Daily News* after the closure. She was a local who worked close by, in the Sixteenth and Suburban Station building.

Though the block had been successful, the owner of the building and its neighboring buildings evicted tenants in 2005 to make way for a thirty-three-story condominium that would spill over the bakery's original landmark and onto neighboring parcels.

44
Italiano's Water Ice

2551 South Twelfth Street

Smack in the middle of a residential part of South Philadelphia's Lower Moyamensing is a walk-up window, where during humidity-drenched Philadelphia summers the Italiano family has been scooping water ice since the 1970s. They don't have a phone number and don't open every summer, and when they do it, they follow their own schedule. Some years it is open in spring; others they debut in July. If open, it closes by August or September if it is a particularly hot summer.

It is one of those places that South Philadelphians only know about and try to keep a secret.

The family-run South Philly landmark claims the title, per its outside signage, of "home of the original gelati." As the story goes, back in 1970, the matriarch of the family, Nora, put water ice and ice cream together and decided to call it *gelati*.

"She decided to call it gelati, originating from the Italian word *gelato*," Nanci Italiano said, the daughter of the shop's originators. "The 'i' is for Italiano. We should have called it 'Savina' instead, or trademarked gelati." (Nora got the idea of mixing water ice and ice cream together from her mom, who enjoyed mixing the two from a nearby shop.)

Nanci continued, "We are definitely the original. Anyone [else] using the gelati name is just playing follow the leader."

What makes Italiano's signature summer treat different is that it uses real ice cream instead of the soft serve like many places do. Italiano's also was proud of using real fruit juice in its water ice, which was always evident by the crates of fresh fruit you could see piled outside. The water ice was sweet but not sugary. It was frozen but also easily slurped.

Water ice—pronounced "wooder" by locals—was a treat that originated from Italian immigrants who were recreating the granita commonly served in their native land. Many Italian immigrants settled first in South Philly, so it was no surprise that the neighborhood was flush with water ice shops.

Lemon and cherry were Italiano's premier flavors. Eventually, it built up its icy repertoire to more than twenty flavors, including favorites such as iced tea, watermelon, peach and a ginger ale creation. Regulars raved about the piña colada flavor and even recommended you come with your own rum to mix in.

The place developed legions of passionate fans, including one on Yelp who imagined that in the year 2021 developed countries would drop five million tons of Italiano's water ice on warring countries to inspire peace. Some also say it holds significant legitimacy from the fact that Nora's husband's father was said to have started selling shaved ice and syrup from a pushcart and later opened Pop's, which was another South Philly water ice institution.

A look at Italiano's Water Ice walk-up window, serving water ice prepared with real fresh fruit juice. *Courtesy of Italiano's Water Ice Facebook.*

Holly Moore wrote that it was pretzels that brought him to Italiano's the first time. "Word had it they are the best around," he wrote. "I showed up sometime around 3 p.m. The nice lady behind the counter welcomed my order with, 'great timing. The second bake pretzels just came out of the oven.' First bake happens in the morning. Really good pretzels."

After the shop's founder passed, her husband, Domenick, and children, Frank, Donna and Nanci, continued her legacy. "We make it with love," Nanci said. "It's just like everything else. It's the right ingredients and enough of the right ingredients."

The summer Frank died suddenly, in early 2013, Italiano's never opened. Nanci and Domenick reopened in 2014, 2015 and 2016, keeping an odd schedule. The open and close dates are dependent on the weather, and the span between them is only four months.

When Italiano's reopened after a 2013 hiatus for its thirty-eighth summer, tears of joy were shed throughout the city. Some called it the best water ice in Philadelphia, the country, the world.

Domenick would contribute to the day-to-day operation of hand-squeezing each lemon. And when he's not working, he sits out front to chat with the frequent customers. With the name attached to the stand, it means family members will always be behind its operation.

Domenick even told Nanci it was okay to let the stand go. And some summers she does. But the prospect of delighting her neighbors was too strong. She may not know all of her customers by name, but she does know what flavor water ice they get.

In 2021, the South Philadelphia community was saddened over the news of Domenick's passing. He was ninety years old. "He'd be outside singing. He could carry a tune. A cappella. He loved talking to the people. He loved making his water ice," Nanci shared with the *Inquirer* after her father's death. "They'd say, 'How do you make it?' He'd say, 'I make it with *love.*'" Many regulars came out of the woodwork over the news, proclaiming his nickname "The Ice Man!" upon hearing the news. "He would have liked that," his daughter said.

Will Italiano's open next year? "Who knows what could happen next year?" said Nanci. "Water ice was always supposed to be a summer thing and a novelty."

PART XI

SERIAL RESTAURATEURS
WITH RESTAURANTS PAST

#

45

Neil Stein, son of a grocer from Mount Airy and a semipro baseball player in his youth, was identified as a "trailblazing, jet-setting restaurateur who helped ignite a sleepy Center City dining scene and brought sidewalk dining to Rittenhouse Square."

His career spanned decades, through restaurant destinations like Mimi Says, Fish Market, Marabella's, Rock Lobster, Striped Bass and Rouge 98.

"He began the real renaissance of Center City," Stephen Starr told the *Inquirer*. "Without Rouge [which opened in 1998], there would have been no Parc. Rittenhouse Square was barren."

"He was the man who made restaurants a destination before food and restaurants were cool," said Philadelphia restaurateur Michael Schulson. "He was the man that paved the road for people like myself and Starr to be able to do what we do in this city."

In late 2001, his empire started to fall apart when the bank and tax authorities came calling. In 2018, he passed, but his legacy continues. His greatest hits are identified below.

MIMI SAYS

At the ripe age of twenty-five, Stein was working selling men's clothing, but he wanted more. With $5,000 from his dad and backing from some others, he opened a supper club in a high rise and named it after his oldest daughter,

Neil Stein, a serial Philadelphia restaurateur, had a career that spanned multiple decades, owning such restaurants as Mimi Says, Fish Market, Marabella's, Rock Lobster, Striped Bass and Rouge 98. *Courtesy of the* Philadelphia Inquirer.

Mimi. At its height, the restaurant grossed $25,000 a week. Due to his frivolous lifestyle, fueled by driving a Jaguar and taking impromptu booze trips to Vegas, things came crashing down, including his first restaurant, by 1971.

FISH MARKET

In 1973, at Eighteenth and Sansom Streets, he debuted Fish Market, which had a fish counter that was a homage to Moe Stein's shop, the Fruit Basket on Wadsworth Avenue. On the day his father died, construction began for his second spin at restaurant ownership. At first, the Fish Market was open for lunch only. Eventually, it grew from 18 to 140 seats, and by 1976, it was making $2.5 million a year. Here was where he developed his reputation as a Philadelphia restaurateur.

In 1981, way before its time, Stein opened a charcuterie spot in Bala Cynwyd, called Icehouse, and then two years later, Marabella's chain partnered with him to expand its business. In 1991, three moneyed partners came to Stein about a pier on the Delaware Riverfront. Rock Lobster effectively created a new destination for outdoor destination dining.

STRIPED BASS

In 1993, Stein's childhood buddy Joe Wolf called with the idea for a restaurant near the Philadelphia Museum of Art. Wolf had recently closed Corned Beef Academy, a modest deli chain for which Stein had written the early menus as a favor. "There's something here big enough for the both of us," Wolf recalled.

Seemingly with no one interested in backing them, the duo went to a group of Orthodox Jews in New York and sold their plan for a first-class seafood restaurant in the building the group owned in Philadelphia. It worked—they walked away with $600,000 to get started. That deal at 2601 Parkway did not happen, but the Butcher & Singer brokerage house at Fifteenth and Walnut Streets was available.

"He made Philadelphia a more cosmopolitan place," said Alison Barshak, the opening chef at Striped Bass.

The same year Striped Bass opened, it was named the "nation's best new restaurant" by *Esquire* and would gross upward of $5.5 million annually by the time 1995 hit.

Stein continued to build on his success for a few years, anyway. In 1999, he revived Fish Market on Eighteenth Street near Sansom, next door to the former Fish Market.

In July 2000, he opened Bleu next door to Rogue, and in late 2000, he took the northwest corner of Broad and Spruce Streets for a grand restaurant called Avenue B.

The crowds never materialized for Avenue B, and Mr. Stein found himself in a hole.

Starr, meanwhile, bid $1.3 million in bankruptcy court to buy Striped Bass. Starr reopened it with the same name in early 2004.

46

Stephen Starr

Philadelphia Inquirer's Karen Heller wrote that restaurateur Stephen Starr is a "cool hunter. He seizes the new. He realized that in a city of neighborhoods, people want the opposite of home. Starr gives his patrons a flight from the familiar." Annette John-Hall, also of the *Inquirer*, added he was the "Quentin Tarantino of nightlife. Starr knows how to attract people. And buzz. He scripts lavish designs and food."

The concert promoter turned restaurant owner's philosophy has worked the majority of the time. (Prior to his spin into restaurants, he even promoted world-renowned comedians like Larry David and Jerry Seinfeld at his South Street comedy club, Stars, in the '80s.) He's introduced the hippest dining rooms in the city, dressed like movie sets, and offered unique experiences along with the finest cocktails.

Starr sees restaurants before he tastes them. He goes to hip places in other cities, or countries, and then hires those designers to build his new restaurant. His favorite word when speaking of his restaurants is "sexy"—promising his restaurants would provide something unlike the normal.

In 2004, he was quoted suggesting: "I looked at this city that I lived in and said, 'there's nowhere that I want to go. There's nowhere I can have any fun.' And so, I made these restaurants." He's shown the city another level of glitz and drama, and he stokes excitement even by the mention of a next project.

"Starr loves the planning, the dreaming, the conception, the anticipation," wrote Heller. "If he were a woman, he'd always be pregnant."

He pushed concepts across the spectrum until one stuck. *Inquirer*'s Craig LaBan once reported his eyes would roll each time he heard what concept Starr would be tackling next. For those that didn't stick, they left Philadelphians with raw emotions, eager for his next project to fill their dining and nightlife voids.

Here follows an overview of several restaurants of his that were once short-lived hits.

Stephen Starr, Philadelphia's "cool hunter," has clocked a delicious track record of restaurants with elaborate cultural experiences unlike any other. *Courtesy of* Philadelphia Magazine.

THE RUSSIAN-INSPIRED CAFÉ REPUBLIC, 1996

Café Republic was Starr's first restaurant he had to close, situated at Twenty-Second and South Streets. Inspired to re-create a Russian martini bar in Philadelphia, Starr introduced an ultra-droll and unique bar specializing in forty-some vodkas, a cigarette menu (it was the '90s) and shot flights in bergs of ice. The intent was to create a watering hole where you could have a light dinner or even a spoonful of caviar while dressed casually, in jeans and a T-shirt.

The food menu was authentic Russian, layered with stuffed cabbage, filet stroganoff, salmon with corn blini pancakes and crème fraiche and pierogis, of course—this time, however, with a side of caviar.

It was fun while it lasted but ultimately a hard sell. A Starbucks now calls the location home.

THE FRENCH-INFLUENCED BLUE ANGEL (2003) BECOMES THE ITALIAN-FOCUSED ANGELINA (2004), ITALIAN TAKE TWO IL PITTORE (2011)

Angelina, a sultry red Italian, triumphed from the failure of Blue Angel. The elegant French bistro, with its nickel-plated bar and twinkling stained-glass ceiling, never garnered the attention that Starr had hoped for, and he didn't skip a beat or wait for the clientele to come before reinventing the restaurant with a $600,000 facelift.

Chef Chris Painter's fried calamari danced in olive-tomato broths, grilled rosemary sausage graced a mound of lentils and Portugal-sourced sardines draped over panzanella salad. Truffle-infused bucatini carbonara and cheese-filled cappelletti delighted diners, as did fork-tender veal tenderloin with fava beans or even rabbit cacciatore. Angelina was capable of filling the void between casual Italian BYOBs and the posh gastronomic Vetri.

Following the success of Angelina, Starr and Painter partnered on a second act, Il Pittore, a semi-eponymous restaurant to the chef. Through its four years in business, the luxe Northern Italian restaurant earned the *Inquirer*'s three bells and three stars from *Philly Mag* and landed on every issue of the magazine's "50 Best Restaurants." The location later became The Love restaurant, a Starr project with Aimee Olexy.

THE MOROCCAN DELIGHT TANGERINE, 1999

In 1999, Stephen Starr debuted his moody Tangerine on Second and Market Streets. It was an ultra-hip expression of Moroccan casbah, with lush draperies, dramatic candle-lit lighting, a granite-colored slate tile floor and dark brown leather tables.

Chris Painter helped the restaurant earn three bells within its first year, with Craig LaBan reporting that Tangerine "is proof that serious restaurants can also be fun." His renditions of traditional Moroccan dishes would arrive in gorgeous Northern African pottery. Flaky *bisteeya* pie was filled with sweet-and-spicy chicken, classic tagine stews were ladled over heaps of couscous and slow-cooked chicken was laden with sour green olives and preserved lemons. "Painter [used] exotic flavors of Morocco and the Mediterranean as a springboard for inventive and skillfully crafted dishes from traditional tagines to spicy riffs on gnocchi and calamari," LaBan relayed in the *Inquirer*. Kevin Lundell's wine list mirrored the chef's inspiration, concentrating on old-world wines, along with a respectable number of new-world vintages.

Starr's most romantic and intimate restaurant, Tangerine was held in high regard as a place that helped to inspire the early adopter of the restaurant scene and developed Starr's old school groupies.

In 2010, Starr called it quits on Tangerine, fearing backlash after 9/11, and decided to re-conceptualize it as Mediterranean. Eventually, the space became Kick Axe Throwing.

A SECOND, MORE CASUAL SEAFOOD SPINNER ROUTE 6, 2011

For two and a half years, Starr backed a well-received New England–inspired seafood restaurant on the stretch of North Broad Street that was a bit of a surprise for most. It was on the same block as Vetri's now defunct Alla Spina and Joe Volpe's catering and event center, Vie.

It brought a much-needed nautical escape to its neighborhood of Mount Vernon, albeit too Joe's Crab, with a bright neon crab on its exterior. It felt like you were in a Cape Cod crab shack, with inspired drink names like the Fairweather, the Nor'Easter and the Cape Codder. Complimentary house-made oyster crackers were brought to you as a treat, and yes, there were lobster bibs.

Ultimately the location didn't work for Starr, and in March 2014 he closed up shop. The Bynum brothers' South Jazz Kitchen now fills its place.

THE CASUAL CONTENDER, SQUARE BURGER, 2009

Similar to Shake Shack in Madison Square Park, Starr introduced his version of quality, fast-casual burgers and shakes in Franklin Square Park in 2009. It was an instant summertime hit, with Cake Shakes swirled with Tastykake Krimpets stealing the show. In 2016, Cooperage, the Cescaphe-backed wine and whiskey bar, took over ownership of the burger shack.

Beginning in 1995, the following restaurants opened under Starr's regime, all of which are open as of this writing and some in partnership with notable Philadelphia chefs: The Continental Restaurant and Martini Bar, Buddakan, Pod (now KPod), Morimoto, El Vez, The Continental Midtown, Barclay Prime, Parc, Butcher and Singer, Pizzeria Stella, El Rey, The Dandelion, Talula's Garden, Frankford Hall, Fette Sau, Serpico, Talula's Daily and The Love. Starr additionally has restaurants in New York City, South Florida, Atlantic City, Washington, D.C., and Paris.

47

Daniel Stern

In 2002, Cherry Hill–bred Daniel Stern landed on Philadelphia's restaurant scene with a gig at Le Bec-Fin. He was actually the first American to be hired by Georges Perrier to run the legendary kitchen. That was a weird time for the restaurant, having been demoted in the Mobil Travel Guide from five to four stars. Perrier was in a tizzy and later dismissed Stern after twenty months. (Though Stern helped him regain his star.)

Stern's recognition from his Bec-Fin days helped him develop a following, and locals cheered for him as he went to open his first restaurant of his own, Gayle. From then, through 2020, he opened celebrated restaurants, earning himself acclaim like being named one of *Philly Mag*'s top restaurants and a nod from *Esquire*'s 2007 best-new restaurant list.

GAYLE

First came Gayle, a thirty-something-seat bistro in Queen Village with intelligent cooking. Named for his wife Jennifer's middle name, the restaurant was upscale, but approachable, where you'd find foie gras next to fries. He'd serve lobster rolls with lavender and a kale pesto, "winter wings" marinated in crème fraiche and lemon, crab dumplings in a buttery broth and crisp risotto with black truffle and soy.

Every dinner was a culinary journey and vibrant experience, with a menu naming only the dish's ingredients, and left patrons guessing what their dinner really would look like before it hit their tabletops. *Courier Post*'s Adam Erace relayed in an early review, "The 'tuna, lime and octopus ceviche' sounded tame enough but not at Gayle. Here, Stern paired the tuna with—no it can't be, that's not, is it—ice cream?" And it was a basmati rice–flavored ice cream served atop the ceviche. Over time, locals developed a bit of fanfare for the deconstructed veal stew, which included a montage of seared, braised, ground parts, sweetbreads and tongue.

After five successful years, Stern closed Gayle to focus on his two imminent restaurants to come: MidAtlantic and R2L.

"While this is certainly a bittersweet decision, we have some very exciting projects to focus on in the immediate future," Stern told the now defunct *Philadelphia City Paper*. "The elements that made Gayle so beloved will definitely play major roles in our new restaurants."

RAE

One year later came Rae, Gayle's more mainstream younger sister, anchoring the lobby of the Cira Center in University City with seats for 220, including a 6-seat wine room and a 10-seat chef's table. The space was mostly fueled by Cira Center workers and Amtrak travelers who feasted over two-dollar martini happy hours and smoked rabbit nachos and crab-and-apple dumplings. It was hard to garner a dinnertime following beyond that, and it closed in 2009. Jose Garces went on to open JG Domestic in its place.

MIDATLANTIC

In 2009, Stern debuted his take on regional American tavern grub on the ground floor of the Science Center in University City. His mission was to spotlight local ingredients executed via modernized heritage dishes that were born in the region. During the time when Stern debuted the concept, descriptors like *farm-to-table*, *regional*, *seasonal* and *local* were becoming overused buzzwords. He differentiated himself by specializing in Pennsylvania cuisine, and his ingredients (e.g., Country Time Farm pork from Berks County) reflected that. He visited farm markets and byways of Dutch country to establish his focus and vibe.

Options like crab scrapple, pretzel chips with horseradish-cheddar dip, saffron noodles, tart sauerkraut, apple fritters and root beer sticky buns impressed thoroughbred Pennsylvania Dutch and intrigued those who perhaps never had scrapple in their lifetime. Drinks were inspired, like the Schuylkill Fish House Punch, a recipe that dated back to 1848; or the Rumspringa, a mash-up of rye, unfiltered apple cider, bitter and honey. In February 2012, Stern announced he was closing MidAtlantic, citing that he was helping the building owners find a replacement operator.

R2L

Perched atop the thirty-seventh floor of Two Liberty Place with panoramic million-dollar views of the city was Daniel Stern's swankiest restaurant. Stern, in his chef's whites, could be found in the elegant kitchen, which was on display through its glass enclosure. Guests saw glimmers of restaurants past in his menu, from Gayle's deconstructed veal stew or Rae's mini Ruebens evolved for the cocktail party crowd.

R2L became known for its lavish parties, kicking off its first event on New Year's Eve 2009.

"Simply getting there is part of the allure," *Inquirer* critic Craig LaBan wrote in 2010 in a stinging one-bell rating.

Chef Daniel Stern, during his time at his restaurant R2L atop the Shops at Liberty Place in Center City Philadelphia. *Courtesy of StarChefs.*

Diners passed through a discreet hallway in the Liberty Two lobby, stepped into a dedicated elevator, then—whoosh! The doors open onto Snazzyville. The swelling buzz of a crowd leads you around the corner, and then the room opens up onto the lounge, where a hive of slinky party dresses and pinstripe suits sip classic cocktails while the setting sun melts like a maraschino cherry over the western horizon.

After a decade's run, R2L announced it was closing during the summer of 2020, one of the many restaurant victims of the coronavirus.

48

Kevin Sbraga

When Kevin Sbraga auditioned for Bravo's *Top Chef* in 2009, he was unemployed and didn't have a car. The Willingboro, New Jersey native was a seasoned chef, having worked for Georges Perrier, Jose Garces and Stephen Starr. Being cast in the highly watched chef competition was his start to better days, and then, when he won the *Top Chef* season 7 title after a fourteen-episode battle against sixteen nationwide competitors, the once down-on-his-luck chef was quickly catapulted to success.

SBRAGA

One year later, on October 15, 2011, with the help of his $125,000 *Top Chef* cash prize, Sbraga debuted his eponymous restaurant on South Broad Street in the Symphony House. The luxe sixty-five-seat dining room was limited to a forty-five-dollar four-course prix fixe arrangement, which, over its time, stole diners' hearts with its signature dish of silky, decadently rich foie gras soup garnished with a delicate rose petal relish and vanilla-poached pears. It was a soup that *everyone* talked about. Its inspiration came by way of a former Philadelphia Eagle, Winston Justice.

"I knew he was into food, so I wanted to make him something new and different," relayed Sbraga to *Food & Wine*. "I had some small foie gras pieces that weren't big enough to sear, so I thought I'd try to make a soup with

Bravo's *Top Chef* winner Kevin Sbraga, known in Philadelphia for his former restaurants, namesake Sbraga and Fat Ham. *Courtesy of Sbraga & Company.*

them, and garnished the soup with rose petals." After that, he couldn't take it off the menu.

Through Sbraga's first year, the chef nabbed regional and national press, with *Philadelphia Magazine*'s critic Trey Popp in 2012 recounting numerous dishes he'd want to order twice, from the cider miso–glazed black cod accented with bok choy and kimchi or the bacon adzuki beans bearing a single cilantro leaf. As he reported, "Sbraga more often showed a rare ability to make the smallest detail stand out."

Philadelphia Inquirer's Craig LaBan is a bit less forgiving, expressing in 2012 that if the restaurant would, "Pause. Edit. Rewind. Play those episodes again. Someday soon, the Sbraga show, with a little more rehearsal, still has a chance to become as good as it appeared on TV." LaBan did, however, grant him three bells, a victory that many Philadelphians strive for, advocating that Sbraga was "finely wrought, evocative, and [with] unique flavors."

But by the end of 2012, *Philly Magazine* named it the fifth-best restaurant in the city, and *Esquire* named it a best new restaurant in America.

Then, by the close of 2013, Sbraga had introduced his second restaurant: southern-inspired, fried chicken–slinging Fat Ham. Situated in University City on the Left Bank of Walnut Street, Sbraga loosened up his menu through comfort food dishes like mac and cheese, collard greens and fried chicken. Before opening, he even took his kitchen crew on a ten-day road trip down south to get utterly immersed in southern cuisine, hitting Louisiana, Alabama, Tennessee and South Carolina.

Of course, another selling point of Fat Ham was also its southern-inspired cocktails, like the blackberry jam mint julep, which included a hearty dose of blackberry jam swirled with a pour of Four Roses Yellow Label bourbon and fresh mint.

Then came the short-lived Juniper Commons, a retro American restaurant at Broad and South Streets that flamed out in six months. "Once we opened the second [restaurant], a lot of opportunities came in," Sbraga said in retrospect of how his series of restaurants were introduced so fast. There was another one too, Sbraga & Co.—a restaurant in Jacksonville, Florida, that he oversaw in a management deal that lasted less than a year—and a second Fat Ham, in the King of Prussia Mall.

Fat Ham continues to be held in many Philadelphians' hearts for its hot chicken, but the memories are bittersweet. The *Top Chef* winner said of his story to *Philadelphia Magazine*, "Ultimately, I grew too fast and wasn't prepared for what I had in front of me."

Fat Ham Recipe: Hot Chicken
Adapted from the recipe published in *Today*, 2016

9 cups buttermilk
2 chickens, cut into pieces
Canola oil, for frying

Dredge
6 cups self-rising flour
6 tablespoons salt
3 tablespoons onion powder
3 tablespoons garlic powder
3 teaspoons smoked paprika

Paste
1 ½ cups lard
6 tablespoons cayenne
3 tablespoons salt
6 teaspoons garlic powder
6 teaspoons onion powder

Serving
4–6 slices brioche bread
Pickle slices
Buttermilk ranch
Dill, chopped

Pour buttermilk into a large bowl. Submerge chicken in buttermilk and let marinate in refrigerator for 15 minutes.

Meanwhile, combine all dredge ingredients in a bowl. Mix well to ensure even seasoning. Remove marinated chicken from refrigerator. Dredge in seasoned flour and allow to sit for 10 minutes.

Make the paste by melting lard at medium heat in a saucepan. Carefully pour lard into a mixing bowl. Add remaining paste ingredients, mix and allow to cool to 100 degrees or room temperature.

Heat canola oil in a deep fryer, wok or deep-walled saucepan to 325 degrees. Working in batches, lower the chicken into the fryer and fry about 12 minutes or until crispy. Remove with slotted spoon. Fill a baster with the paste and squeeze it over the chicken right out of the fryer.

Arrange bread slices on a platter. Top with pickles, buttermilk ranch and dill for a cooling effect and finish with hot chicken on top. Serve immediately.

Bibliography

Adamson, April, and Rose DeWolf. "Lack of Space Forces Closure of Rindelaub's, a Rittenhouse Square Institution." *Philadelphia Daily News*, December 5, 2002.

Allyn, Bobby. "Customers Say Goodbye to Little Pete's, One of the Last All-Night Diners in Center City." *WHYY*, May 26, 2017. https://whyy.org/articles/customers-say-goodbye-to-little-petes-one-of-the-last-all-night-diners-in-center-city/.

Andries de Groot, Roy. "One Great Dish: Apple Tart with Chocolate Mousse." *Courier-Post*, June 17, 1981.

Armstrong, Jenice. "Relish the Thought: Owners of the Legendary Zanzibar Blue Are About to Open a New Spot." *Philadelphia Daily News*, February 10, 2009.

Binzen, Peter. "Son Follows Father's Restaurant Success with Pearl of his Own." *Philadelphia Inquirer*, April 11, 1997.

Broussard, Meredith. "Return of the Neon Hot Dog: Old Original Levi's Hot Dog Sign to Be Relit on South Street." Hidden City Philadelphia, July 18, 2012. https://hiddencityphila.org/2012/07/return-of-the-neon-hot-dog-old-original-levis-hot-dog-sign-to-be-relit-on-south-street/.

Burros, Marian. "A Restaurant Revival in the City of Brotherly Love." *Washington Post*, June 14, 1979. https://www.washingtonpost.com/archive/lifestyle/1979/06/14/a-restaurant-revival-in-the-city-of-brotherlylove.

Bykofsky, Stu, and Sono Motoyama. "Neil Stein Files for Bankruptcy." *Philadelphia Daily News*, March 11, 2003.

Cavallo, Craig. "Chefs and Food Luminaries on How Philadelphia's Le Bec-Fin Changed American Fine Dining." *Saveur*, February 25, 2016. https://www.saveur.com/king-georges-le-bec-fin-documentary.

Chastain, Sue. "Strolli's: Plain and Inexpensive but Such Satisfying Italian Fare." *Philadelphia Inquirer*, March 6, 1981.

Clark, Lisa. "Defunct Philly Eateries Linger in Form of 'Frog/Commissary' Recipes." *Trib Live*, March 3, 2002. https://archive.triblive.com/news/defunct-philly-eateries-linger-in-form-of-frog-commissary-recipes/.

Collins, Bill. "Black Banana Rates High, Takes a Bunch of Money." *Philadelphia Inquirer*, March 19, 1976.

———. "Down with Diets, They're Dining with Gusto Again." *Philadelphia Inquirer*, October 17, 1979.

———. "Fine Restaurants in Philadelphia Starve for Customers." *Philadelphia Inquirer*, October 3, 1976.

———. "Glorious Adventure…No Wonder, Meal Cost $75." *Philadelphia Inquirer*, August 24, 1975.

———. "La Panetiere: After 12 Years, It's Still the Most Impressive." *Philadelphia Inquirer*, October 5, 1979.

———. "Young La Truffe Chef Doing Well, Thank You." *Philadelphia Inquirer*, April 5, 1974.

Collins, Glenn. "The Automat May Be Long Gone, But Its Recipes Are in Demand." *New York Times*, December 17, 2012.

Cook, Bonnie L. "Kathleen Mulhern, Owner of The Garden, which Sparked Philly's Early Restaurant Renaissance." *Philadelphia Inquirer*, February 8, 2019. https://www.inquirer.com/obituaries/the-garden-kathleen-mulhern-restaurant-renaissance-spruce-street-20190208.html.

Corr, John. "After 50 Years of Steaks, Arthur's." *Philadelphia Inquirer*, June 8, 1982.

———. "Ex-Waiter to Reopen Former Arthur's Steak House as Arturo's." *Philadelphia Inquirer*, October 14, 1986.

Costantinou, Marianne. "Nightlife: Call Ahead for Cannoli." *Philadelphia Daily News*, December 17, 1987.

Crowley, Carolyn Hughes. "Meet Me at the Automat." *Smithsonian Magazine*, August 2001. https://www.smithsonianmag.com/arts-culture/meet-me-at-the-automat-47804151/.

Curry, Bill. "On the Go: Banana Will Appeal to After-Theater Set." *Philadelphia Inquirer*, March 14, 1978.

D'Addono, Beth. "A Feast for the Eyes." *Courier-Post*, September 28, 1994.

————. "Food Tree: Top Philadelphia Restauranteurs Nurture Next Generation of Fine-Dining Talent." *Philadelphia Inquirer*, August 24, 2011. https://www.inquirer.com/philly/food/20110825_Top_Philadelphia_restaurateurs_nurture_next_generation_of_fine-dining_talent.html.

————. "French Connection: A Culinary Angle Is Included in Philadelphia Flower Show." *Courier-Post*, February 25, 1998.

————. "Philadelphia's 'Gastronomic Anchor.'" *Courier-Post*, September 27, 2000.

Daily Record. "Colonnade Co. Signs Lease in Philadelphia." July 10, 1964.

Daily Register. "Barbecued Cornish Hens '1609.'" August 25, 1982.

Dekom, Otto. "Man Says Delawareans Have Taste: Review Brought Him His 'Just Desserts.'" *News Journal*, October 30, 1975.

Dent, Mark. "Local Beer and Little Pete's: Roadies for Interpol, Bruce Springsteen Share Their Philly Picks." *Billy Penn*, June 23, 2015. https://billypenn.com/2015/06/23/local-beer-and-little-petes-roadies-for-interpol-bruce-springsteen-share-their-philly-picks/.

Erace, Adam. "A Chef's Encore: Jim Burke Was One of Philly's Most Promising Talents." *Philadelphia Inquirer*, December 19, 2019.

————. "Creativity Rules at Daniel Stern's Gayle." *Courier-Post*, April 9, 2006.

————. "Uneven Menu Dulls a Visit to Rae." *Courier-Post*, February 17, 2008.

Etchells, Arthur. "Friday Saturday Sunday Throwing One Last Wine Dinner." *Philadelphia Magazine*, July 2015. https://www.phillymag.com/foobooz/2015/07/23/friday-saturday-sunday-last-wine-dinner/

————. "Meritage Closing After Nine Years." *Philadelphia Magazine*, September 2015. https://www.phillymag.com/foobooz/2015/09/16/meritage-closing-after-nine-years/

Etter, Gerald. "Colonnade Will Serve No More." *Philadelphia Inquirer*, December 16, 1984.

————. "Frankie Bradley's Closed, For Sale." *Philadelphia Inquirer*, October 22, 1986.

————. "Pioneer in Mesquite Grilling Shows That It Still Has the Spark." *Philadelphia Inquirer*, September 14, 1990.

"Everybody went to Bookie's." *Philadelphia Magazine*, May 15, 2006. https://www.phillymag.com/news/2006/05/15/everybody-went-to-bookies/

Fields, Larry. "Bradleys: Stars' Favorite Dish." *Philadelphia Daily News*, September 15, 1983.

————. "Frankie Bradley: Vanishing Tradition." *Philadelphia Daily News*, January 13, 1976.

Fiorillo, Victor. "David Ansill to Expatriate to Jamaica, Smoke Lots of Weed." *Philadelphia Magazine*, January 4, 2012. https://www.phillymag.com/foobooz/2012/01/04/david-ansill-to-expatriate-to-jamaica-smoke-lots-of-weed/

Fisher, Keri. "8 Great Water Ices in Philadelphia." *Gourmet*, June 17, 2009.

Flatt, Collin. "Iconic Chef David Ansill Reflects on Pif, Stephen Starr, and 30 Years on the Line in Philly." *Eater Philadelphia*, January 30, 2012. https://philly.eater.com/2012/1/30/6618447/iconic-chef-david-ansill-reflects-on-pif-stephen-starr-and-30-years.

Fox, Tom. "Curse of Bigness Hits La Banane." *Philadelphia Daily News*, December 10, 1971.

Giordano, Rita. "Domenick Italiano, South Philly Water Ice Entrepreneur, Dies at 90." *Philadelphia Inquirer*, June 17, 2021. https://www.inquirer.com/obituaries/domenick-italiano-water-ice-gelati-south-philly-obit-20210617.html.

Gordinier, Jeff. "America's Bocuse Retires in Philadelphia." *New York Times*, March 6, 2012. https://www.nytimes.com/2012/03/07/dining/georges-perrier-of-le-bec-fin-hangs-up-his-toque.html.

Gugino, Sam. "Nightlife: The Aging of Aquarius." *Philadelphia Daily News*, June 14, 1988.

Heick, Frank. "Colonnade on Juniper St. to Close." *Philadelphia Inquirer*, May 20, 1977.

Heller, Karen. "The Fish That Ate Philly." *Philadelphia Inquirer*, September 25, 1994.

Henninger, Danya. "David Ansill's Next Act: Marijuana-Infused Pop-Up Dinners." *Billy Penn*, January 29, 2017. https://billypenn.com/2017/01/29/david-ansills-next-act-marijuana-infused-pop-up-dinners/.

———. "The Spot: Snockey's." *Philadelphia Inquirer*, October 19, 2014. https://www.inquirer.com/philly/blogs/food_department/The-Spot-Snockeys.html.

Henri, Kirsten. "The Revisit: Friday Saturday Sunday." *Philadelphia Magazine*, February 2011. https://www.phillymag.com/foobooz/2011/02/25/the-revisit-friday-saturday-sunday-2/.

Hochman, Stan. "Eats: Two Quails." *Philadelphia Daily News*, November 25, 1983.

Holton, Ray. "Horn & Hardart's, Bain's on S. Broad Street." *Philadelphia Inquirer*, May 7, 1983.

Jones, Alexandra. "14 Great Philly Restaurants We Wish Hadn't Closed." *Philadelphia Magazine*, September 2018. https://www.phillymag.com/foobooz/2018/09/26/best-closed-restaurants-philadelphia/.

Joseph, Gar. "Family Fare: Catch More than Nostalgia." *Philadelphia Daily News*, April 19, 1995.

Kittrels, Alonzo. "Back in the Day: Horn & Hardart's, the Original 'Fast Food.'" *Philadelphia Tribune*, November 4, 2017.

Klein, Michael. "A Change at the Top of Le Bec-Fin." *Philadelphia Inquirer*, February 13, 2012.

———. "Founder of Deja Vu Comes Around Again." *Philadelphia Inquirer*, November 2, 1997.

———. "Italiano's Water Ice Returns in South Philly—Yet Again." *Philadelphia Inquirer*, August 8, 2018. https://www.inquirer.com/philly/blogs/the-insider/italianos-water-ice-returns-south-philly-gelati-20180808.html.

———. "Neil Stein, Trailblazing Restauranteur, Dies at 77." *Philadelphia Inquirer*, October 26, 2018. https://www.inquirer.com/philly/blogs/the-insider/neil-stein-restaurateur-striped-bass-rouge-obituary-20181026.html.

———. "Return of Philippe Chin." *Philadelphia Inquirer*, May 17, 2012. https://www.inquirer.com/philly/blogs/the-insider/The-return-of-Philippe-Chin.html.

———. "R2L, One of Philly's Loftiest Restaurants, Has Closed Permanently, Sources Say." *Philadelphia Inquirer*, June 10, 2020. https://www.inquirer.com/food/r2l-daniel-stern-two-liberty-place-high-restaurant-closed-20200610.html.

———. "Ty Bailey, Pioneering Knave of Hearts Restaurant Owner and Swim Coach, Has Died at 69." *Philadelphia Inquirer*, March 1, 2021. https://www.inquirer.com/obituaries/ty-bailey-knave-of-hearts-restaurant-obituary-20210301.html.

Krall, Hawk. "Hot Dog of the Week: Philly Combo." *Serious Eats*, June 23, 2009. https://www.seriouseats.com/2009/06/hot-dog-of-the-week-philly-combo-philadelphia-pepper-hash-levis.html.

LaBan, Craig. "Dear Georges Perrier: What the Bec Has Happened?" *Philadelphia Inquirer*, February 4, 2012. https://www.inquirer.com/philly/food/20120205_le_bec.html.

———. "Dining Review: James." *Philadelphia Inquirer*, May 6, 2007.

———. "Dining Review: Koo Zee Doo." *Philadelphia Inquirer*, January 17, 2010.

———. "Dining Review: Marigold Kitchen." *Philadelphia Inquirer*, December 13, 2009.

———. "Dining Review: Marigold Kitchen." *Philadelphia Inquirer*, February 6, 2005.

———. "Dining Review: MidAtlantic." *Philadelphia Inquirer*, February 14, 2010.

———. "Dining Review: Sansom Street Oyster House." *Philadelphia Inquirer*, January 23, 2000.

———. "Dining Review: Sbraga." *Philadelphia Inquirer*, January 7, 2012. https://www.inquirer.com/philly/food/20120108_Sbraga_shows_promise__but_service_needs_a_boost.html.

———. "Dining Review: Striped Bass." *Philadelphia Inquirer*, August 15, 1999.

———. "Dining Review: Tashan." *Philadelphia Inquirer*, December 10, 2011. https://www.inquirer.com/philly/food/20111211_Tashan.html

———. "Memories to Savor." *Philadelphia Inquirer*, January 9, 2000.

———. "Philadelphia Dining." *Philadelphia Inquirer*, May 21, 2000.

———. "Ringing in the New Year with a Look Back at 2010." *Philadelphia Inquirer*, December 26, 2010.

———. "Salts of the Earth." *Philadelphia Inquirer*, September 30, 1998.

Landers, Peggy. "Surf & Turf: An Older, Wiser Neil Stein Opens Fishmarket in a Place He Knows Well." *Philadelphia Daily News*, October 21, 1999.

Lawlor, Julia. "Eats: La Truffe." *Philadelphia Daily News*, December 16, 1977.

Lee, Chris. "Chilled Sweet Summer Corn Soup." *Philadelphia Inquirer*, July 28, 2005.

"Like All Good Things, Carman Country Kitchen Is Coming to an End." WHYY, October 3, 2012. https://whyy.org/articles/like-all-good-things-carmans-country-kitchen-is-coming-to-an-end/.

Lobrano, Alexander. "Restaurant Report: Le Bec Fin in Philadelphia." *New York Times*, December 14, 2012. https://www.nytimes.com/2012/12/16/travel/restaurant-report-le-bec-fin-in-philadelphia.html.

Lowe, Frederick. "The End of Line for Another Colonnade." *Philadelphia Daily News*, March 8, 1985.

Ludwig, Elisa. "Principles of Paella." *Philadelphia Inquirer*, August 14, 2014. https://www.inquirer.com/philly/food/20140814_Principles_of_paella.html.

Manning, Joy. "100 Years Shucking Oysters." *Philadelphia Inquirer*, May 3, 2012.

Marter, Marilynn. "Even in a Time of Changing Tastes, the Steakhouse Still Flourishes." *Philadelphia Inquirer*, December 24, 1986.

———. "Strawberries Find a Home in Soup, Pie." *York Daily Record*, June 13, 1990.

Matheson, Kathy. "One for the Books: Penn Acquiring Chef's Huge Gastronomy Collection." *Philadelphia Daily News*, December 9, 2006.

Mathis, Joel. "Meet Little Pete, the Man Who Could Lose His Diner for a Butt-Ugly Hotel." *Philadelphia Magazine*, January 28, 2015. https://www.phillymag.com/news/2015/01/28/little-pete-koutroubas-diner/.

McDonald, Natalie Hope. "The Black Banana Reunion." *Philadelphia Magazine*, January 11, 2011. https://www.phillymag.com/news/2011/01/11/the-black-banana-reunion/.

Melamed, Samantha. "What's Left of Little Pete's? Salvaging Artifacts—and Memories." *Philadelphia Inquirer*, May 30, 2017. https://www.inquirer.com/philly/food/whats-left-of-little-petes-salvaging-artifacts-and-memories-20170530.html

Mom Mom's Apron. "Easiest and Best Cream of Mushroom Soup." October 12, 2012. https://mmapron.com/2012/10/21/easiest-and-best-cream-of-mushroom-soup/.

Moran, Robert. "Fritz Blank, Owner of Deux Cheminees, Dies." *Philadelphia Inquirer*, September 11, 2014. https://www.inquirer.com/philly/obituaries/20140911_Fritz_Blank__owner_of_Deux_Chemines__dies.html.

Morgan, Arlene Notoro. "A Native's Guide to S. Phila. Eating." *Philadelphia Inquirer*, October 5, 1984.

Morgan, Peggy. "He Greets Every Season with Food." *Courier-Post*, May 25, 1980.

Motoyama, Sono. "Review: Marigold Kitchen Glows Bright." *Philadelphia Daily News*, December 17, 2004.

Nichols, Rick. "Deux Cheminees." *Philadelphia Inquirer*, November 14, 2004.

———. "Fish Gotta Fly." *Philadelphia Inquirer*, June 4, 1995.

———. "Good Taste: A Salad Classic Revived." *Philadelphia Inquirer*, March 22, 2012.

———. "Latest Starr in the Firmament: Blue Angel." *Philadelphia Inquirer*, November 17, 1999.

———. "Lobster Roll Redux." *Philadelphia Inquirer*, June 26, 2002.

———. "On the Side: An Oyster House Is at Low Tide." *Philadelphia Inquirer*, June 19, 2008.

———. "On the Side: Transplanting Shank's." *Philadelphia Inquirer*, April 9, 2009. https://www.inquirer.com/philly/food/restaurants/20090409_On_the_Side__Transplanting_Shank_s.html.

———. "Post-Django life." *Philadelphia Inquirer*, April 8, 2007. https://www.inquirer.com/philly/entertainment/20070408_Post-Django_life_of_tasty_possibility.html.

————. "Salad's Days: The Engagingly Retro Milan Shows Staying Power." *Philadelphia Inquirer*, June 2, 2002.

————. "Sweet Survivor: Rindelaub's Is on the Move. Its Secret-Recipe German Chocolate Cake Soldiers On." *Philadelphia Inquirer*, March 18, 2001.

————. "Who'll Save Pepper Hash?" *Philadelphia Inquirer*, April 12, 2009. https://www.inquirer.com/philly/entertainment/20090412_Who_ll_save_pepper_hash_.html.

O'Brien, Jim. "Celebs Still Find Their Way to Frankie Bradley's Old Philly Institution." *Philadelphia Daily News*, November 3, 1972.

Orso, Anna. "Your Little Pete's Stories: From Bathroom Sex to Heart Attack Cabbage." *Billy Penn*, March 22, 2017. https://billypenn.com/2017/03/22/your-little-petes-stories-from-bathroom-sex-to-heart-attack-cabbage/.

Pernot, Guillermo. "Jalapeno-Seafood Fritter Appetizers." *Selma Enterprise*, August 6, 2003.

Philadelphia Daily News. "Restaurateur Peter von Starck." June 27, 1984.

Philadelphia Inquirer. "First-Rate Cafeterias: Just Help Yourself." January 23, 1976.

Philadelphia Jewish Exponent. "Ode to a Beloved Bakery: Hesh's, B.I.P. (Bake in Peace)." January 15, 2014. https://www.jewishexponent.com/2014/01/15/ode-to-a-beloved-bakery-heshs-b-i-p-bake-in-peace/.

Popp, Trey. "Restaurant Review: Sbraga." *Philadelphia Magazine*, January 2012. https://www.phillymag.com/news/2012/01/24/restaurant-review-sbraga/.

Primis, Ashley. "239 Best Dishes to Eat in Philly: Bring It Back!" *Philadelphia Magazine*, December 2009. https://www.phillymag.com/news/2009/12/22/239-best-dishes-to-eat-in-philly-bring-it-back/.

Quinn, Jim. "The Chefs Take Over." *Philadelphia Inquirer*, October 14, 1990.

————. "Look Back at Friday Saturday Sunday's First Review." *Philadelphia Magazine*, August 2015. https://www.phillymag.com/foobooz/2015/08/12/friday-saturday-sunday-first-review/.

Rea, Steven X. "The Succulent Empire of Steven Poses." *Philadelphia Inquirer*, November 11, 1984.

Richberg, Barbara J. "Frank 'Shank' Perri, a Master Italian Cook." *Philadelphia Inquirer*, March 18, 1994.

Robling, Lari. "Koo Zee Doo Means Cooked, Perfectly." *Philadelphia Daily News*, November 20, 2009.

Rothman, Jordana. "How Kevin Sbraga Impressed a Philadelphia Eagle." *Food & Wine*, May 23, 2017. https://www.foodandwine.com/travel/how-kevin-sbraga-impressed-philadelphia-eagle.

Sbraga, Kevin. "Hot Fried Chicken." *Today*, July 28, 2016. https://www.today.com/recipes/hot-fried-chicken-t101228.

Schmidt, Tom. "Family Fare: Bain's Cafeteria." *Philadelphia Daily News*, August 17, 1979.

Schrambling, Regina. "In Philadelphia, a New Taste of Freedom." *New York Times*, March 13, 2002.

Seidman, Andrew. "Hesh's, a Northeast Institution, Closes." *Philadelphia Inquirer*, January 12, 2014.

Shapiro, Howard S. "The Neighborhood Restaurants." *Washington Post*, April 5, 1987.

Snyder, Amanda L. "Scoop of Perfection." *South Philly Review*, March 15, 2012.

Sokolic, William H. "Sandwiches and Success: Chain Built of Corned Beef." *Philadelphia Inquirer*, June 30, 1993.

Solomonov, Michael. "Fenugreek Braised Short Ribs." *Philadelphia Inquirer*, November 1, 2007.

Stephens, Regan. "46 Years In, This Philly Restaurant Finally Hit Its Stride." *Food & Wine*, April 23, 2019. https://www.foodandwine.com/travel/restaurants/friday-saturday-sunday-philadelphia.

Stevens, William K. "After a Decade, an Adventure in Dining Out; From A to B and More." *New York Times*, May 21, 1986.

———. "Aging Patrons Seal Restaurants Fate." *New York Times*, November 17, 1987.

Tait, Elaine. "Arthur's Steak House Closes after 54 Years." *Philadelphia Inquirer*, July 22, 1986.

———. "At the New Le Bec-Fin: Almost a 10." *Philadelphia Inquirer*, December 11, 1983.

———. "Chips Are Down: Remembering a Unique Restaurateur." *Philadelphia Inquirer*, June 27, 1984.

———. "Foie Gras Season's Here." *Philadelphia Inquirer*, October 8, 1980.

———. "From Europe, New Delights." *Philadelphia Inquirer*, September 5, 1979.

———. "Let Them Eat Carrot Cake." *Philadelphia Inquirer*, June 1, 1980.

———. "Light at the Top of the Stairs." *Philadelphia Inquirer*, June 17, 1979.

———. "Nouvelle Cuisine: French Food with a Fresh Approach." *Philadelphia Inquirer*, September 17, 1978.

————. "Pace Suits You to a Tea." *Philadelphia Inquirer*, May 26, 1972.

————. "Simply Superb: Bay Scallops in Gin Cream Sauce." *Philadelphia Inquirer*, June 6, 1982.

————. "To This Chef, an $18 Meal Is a Gourmet Bargain." *Philadelphia Inquirer*, May 23, 1973.

————. "Weekend Dines Out and Likes It." *Philadelphia Inquirer*, March 2, 1971.

Teel, Emily. "First Look: Inside the New Friday Saturday Sunday." *Philadelphia Magazine*, January 1, 2017. https://www.phillymag.com/foobooz/2017/01/16/first-look-inside-the-new-friday-saturday-sunday/.

Tewfik, Alex. "Marigold Kitchen to Close Its Doors for Good in West Philly." *Philadelphia Magazine*, January 26, 2019. https://www.phillymag.com/foobooz/2019/01/26/marigold-kitchen-closing-west-philadelphia/.

Williams, Edgar. "Restoring Tea Room with Style." *Philadelphia Inquirer*, March 28, 1980.

About the Author

Amy Strauss is a food marketer by day and a food writer by night. She's the author of *Pennsylvania Scrapple: A Delectable History* (The History Press, 2017) and has clocked over a decade of experience in food writing, advertising and content partnerships, including those with well-known brands such as Campbell Soup Company, Wawa, Disney, Hallmark Channel, Universal Music Group, *Bon Appétit*, *Good Morning America* and Open Table. She lives in Philadelphia and owns Herman's Coffee with her husband, Mat Falco. Follow her on Instagram at @amystrauss or visit her online at amystrauss.com.